But Do They Have
Field Experience!

But Do They Have Field Experience!

Compiled and Edited by
Elayne Clift

with original illustrations by
Kim Winnard

OGN Publications

But Do They Have Field Experience!
Published 1993 by OGN Publications, 11320 Rouen Drive, Potomac, MD 20854
Text Copyright © 1993 Elayne Clift
Illustrations Copyright © 1993 Kim Winnard

Acknowledgments
I am indebted to Kristin Cooney, Kim Winnard, Jenna Dixon, and Krishna Sondhi for helping this vision become a reality.
I also wish to thank the contributors, and all the others who shared their work so generously.
"A Modern Doctor Schweitzer" is reprinted with permission of the *Annals of Internal Medicine.*

Editorial assistance by Kristin Cooney

Production supervised by Jenna Dixon,
   Bookbuilder, 800 377-6825
Cover design by Laura Augustine
Text design by Jenna Dixon
Copyedited by Jolene Robinson
Typeset by Rosanne Pignone, ProProduction
Proofread by Vera Jhung

Printed in the United States of America by McNaughton & Gunn.
Text printed on 50% recycled, acid-free paper with natural oil-based ink.
First Impression 1993.

ISBN 0-9634827-0-X

Dedication

For my friend Elson in Malawi, and for the Elsons everywhere.

CONTENTS

Preface   *ix*

CHAPTER 1 **LATIN AMERICA AND THE CARIBBEAN**   **1**
           "The Bleeding Heart Health Spa"

           The New York Connection   5
           The Prophet   8
           Two Weeks in Rosario   10
           Bocaraca   25
           All Jerson Needed Was a Chance   27
           Cuernavaca   29
           Passages   30
           An Old Story   35
           Letters Home   49

CHAPTER 2 **AFRICA**   **53**
           "Who Taught Those Chickens How To Swim?"

           A Village Visit   57
           José   61
           Soul to Soul   72
           The Field Librarian   81
           A Drop in the Bucket   85
           Moussa's Table   87
           A Gambian Coup   89
           A Modern Doctor Schweitzer   101
           Letters Home   103

CHAPTER 3   **ASIA AND THE NEAR EAST**   **109**
             "Let Them Only Be Sleeping"

             The Journal   113
             A Friend from New Town Girls' School   116
             Langenscheidt's Lilliput Dictiona   125
             Echoes of Guilt   131
             Shanghai Diary   134
             Letters Home   138

CHAPTER 4 · **IMAGES IN VERSE**   **145**

             Interlude, Afghanistan   149
             A Writer Named Fatimah   150
             The Subramuniyam Temple   152
             Bombay   153
             New Delhi Intercontinental Hotel   154
             Anyanhaseyo Ajumoni—Hello Auntie in
                Korean   155
             Ndutu   157
             Whose Bargain?   158
             First Impressions   159
             And Still the Women Weep   160
             For Sonia   162
             For Marta   164

PREFACE

The seeds for this book were first planted in 1986 in Honduras. A group of us ("gringos") were sitting around the bar at the Hotel Maya having nearly "cashed it in" earlier that day during what—putting it mildly—was a rough landing at the Tegucigalpa airport. One thing led to another, and soon the "war stories" came tumbling out of people, some hysterically funny, some desperately sad, all about real life experiences while working and living in developing countries.

A relative latecomer, I had personally begun to explore working in international development some years earlier. But wherever I went, one question haunted me.

"Do you have any field experience?" Variations on this theme abounded.

"Have you worked overseas?"

"Where have you worked in the developing world?"

"Did you say you've NEVER lived abroad?"

I soon realized that to the experienced internationalist, Nepal was the Scarsdale of Asia, fluency in two languages was hardly impressive, and true credibility rested with a multipaged curriculum vitae listing exotic assignments for large donor agencies like the U.S. Agency for International Development or the World Bank.

My twenty years of professional life suddenly seemed pale, meaningless, and nontransferable. But I was determined, and persistent, and after a heavy dose of networking, traveling, writing, consulting, and otherwise paying my dues, I found my niche in development in the field of health communication.

Then, to my utter amazement, I heard myself not only answering the Ultimate Question, but occasionally asking it myself: "But do you have field experience?"

This book grew out of that pervasive query. It is a tribute to those special people who have been tenacious and committed enough to enter into the world of development, and hopefully it will serve to inspire (or warn) others whose career goals include time in the developing world.

The contributors represented here are ordinary, extraordinary individuals who have brought their skills and energy to bear in a variety of countries, sectors, and circumstances. Some of them are seasoned development "experts," others idealists eager to make their mark. For some, getting overseas was part of a well-planned career. For others, it just happened. But whether Peace Corps volunteer, consultant, spouse, nongovernmental organization (NGO) representative, or resident representative of a major donor, each of them has a story to tell, and an answer to that fundamental question still being asked by development recruiters around the world: "But do they have field experience?"

When I first began to compile the letters, diary and journal entries, short stories, and vignettes that people sent me from all over the world, I felt overwhelmed by the task I had given myself. How would I ever structure the material, give it one "voice"? But as I sorted through the contributions, so rich with reality, I soon realized that there was no need to organize, and little room to edit. The voices were there already, saying eloquently and clearly what there was to be shared; the stories told themselves.

My job has therefore been simply, and with great pleasure, to provide a forum for these rich tales to be told. But do they have field experience? Do they ever!

CHAPTER 1

LATIN AMERICA AND THE CARIBBEAN

"The Bleeding Heart Health Spa"

I am ten pounds lighter, and my skin is a few shades darker. I look like I've been to a health spa, and, in a way, I have—the Bleeding Heart Health Spa, Rosario, Honduras. Sometimes I have felt cynical about this whole project. I've speculated that it's just a way for doctors and architects and lawyers with liberal leanings to think they've "done something."

"Oh, yes," they can say, "I went to Honduras, and worked in a little village there."

"Oh, how wonderful," their friends will reply, "would you like another hors d'oeuvre?"

—Sybil Smith

The New York Connection

William A. Smith

The Indians of Colombia, the Guambiana, are ethnically quite pure. They are directly related to their more famous southern cousins, and have been trapped in this small Colombian valley by five hundred years of progress. The men wear a brilliant blue cloth wrapped around their middle and a tightly woven black *ruana*—very short poncho—just enough to keep out the cold. Their faces are windburned, a phenomenon that seems to bring the blood to the surface of the cheeks and makes them look rather like polished clay. The women are very close-limbed—they move as though they were balancing firewood on their heads, even when they're not. They are not a beautiful people except in the real sense of that word—they are totally adapted to their world.

That world is a valley—one long, river-cut crease in the earth out of which they've chopped foundations for their houses and scraped platforms to bury their potato seed and corn. Rocks here don't just lie around like so much rubble, they grow as an integral part of the earth. Everything is bigger than the people —the river is beyond their control, the mountains look down upon them with a contemptuous self-assurance, and the sky stretches far beyond their capacity to see.

The path itself hung over the river, which poured through a valley some six hundred feet below. As we passed, the women would turn their heads down and respond with a quiet adios,

William A. Smith, Ph.D., is Executive Vice President, The Academy for Educational Development, Washington, D.C. He was formerly with the Peace Corps in Bolivia and Ecuador.

5

never stopping for a moment their making of thread, but always looking back over their shoulder at our strange sight. One particularly curious thing happened as we walked together. Six of the Indians saw the three of us coming and turned, climbed the cliff beside the road, and stared curiously at us as we walked by. I waved to them and called "Adios." They responded and smiled, but I felt then that I knew how Pizarro must have felt: facing people who could not possibly understand they were looking their own future in the face.

After walking for almost ten minutes we came upon a woman whose neck was covered with small strings of white beads. I was fascinated and began to talk to her. She seemed very at ease but I sensed a certain awkwardness between us. She answered all my questions—explained very forcibly that this was not a pueblo, but a *pueblito,* a village, and said she really didn't know what it was called. She directed us, however, to the schoolmaster, who could answer all our questions. As we turned away to leave, she touched my arm and looked me quite squarely in the face and said, *"Ustedes son de lejos—de lejos!"* You are from far away—far away! I remember that impressing me greatly at the time.

The schoolmaster was a man of forty-five. As we approached him, I held out my hand. He responded, although it didn't seem to be his custom. I explained that we were teachers, too, and had come simply to enjoy the beauty around his town. He seemed interested and asked if we would like to see the school. We said yes and were off. Several minutes after leaving the house, he asked where we were from—I thought immediately that the only place he would recognize would be New York. I told him that we lived north of New York. He responded, *"Yo conozo Nueva York."* That didn't surprise me; *conozo* can mean anything from I've heard of it to I've been there before. Then he said, "I was there for fourteen days!" Here at the end of a valley literally forgotten by the last five centuries—a man, looking like all the other men—told me he had enjoyed his visit to New York but would not want to live there!

We became friends, I think. We asked him questions and he asked us questions. He was born in this valley—studied weaving in Popayan and returned to be a teacher. After ten years of teaching he went to Bogota. There he was discovered by the U.S. Agency for International Development and sent to Ecuador to study more about weaving. He then went to the New York World Fair and was there for fourteen days demonstrating Colombian weaving. He flew in a jet, he told me.

Francisco returned to his pueblo, where he has one classroom with two grades—twenty-seven children—and one blackboard. Pictures of the Colombian great men and a painting of a bleeding Santa Elizabeth emphasized the emptiness that surrounded them. Francisco said he enjoyed teaching, but the children were very timid. He did not teach them Spanish; he taught them Castillano.

We went to his home and we talked about him and about his town. He had two school certificates on the wall, as well as a Colombia-Gothic portrait of his parents, several small pictures, and a framed photograph of the Capitol Building in Washington, D.C. One whole side of his house was an altar, complete with two large female saints and draped with the flag of Colombia and the flag of a saint.

We had coffee, talked, exchanged addresses, and left. I decided to send Francisco some books for his school, and he became a very pleasant, very warm, memory.

I suppose there should be a moral to this kind of story—but there isn't to this one. We left the Callejon de Guambiano as we had found it.

The Prophet

Sarah Handlin Milner

I heard Tyrone long before I saw him. His great baritone boomed out through the quiet rustle of trees and reached me where I stood in front of the church in St. Lawrence Gap. I walked toward the sound of his voice.

"We all sinners. Repent before it be too late!"

I came through the curve in the Gap and passed the South Winds Hotel and the group of taxi drivers playing their incessant games of dominoes. The voice called out and I followed it across the entrance to the Southern Palms. Finally I found him under a coconut palm, seated on a folding chair at the side of the road, not far from the branch office of the Barclay's Bank. He had spread a red cotton cloth over a wooden box, and on this makeshift display case he exhibited his wood carvings.

He was a big black man with a head of greying woolly hair that reached out about his head like a black and silver halo. His bright smile flashed out at me even as he finished his prophetic flow of rhetoric, warning of the evils of mankind and the just punishment that would soon be meted out to the wicked world.

"The Lord sees you and me," he shouted.

He was quiet when I picked up one of his carvings and studied it. He fixed his eyes on my face and a look of pride and

Sarah Handlin Milner is an economist with a background that includes years of work with the International Monetary Fund and with the Organization of American States. She is the first woman chosen to direct a field office of the OAS and served for seven years in Barbados, where her story is based. She is the mother of two daughters and now teaches economics at the University of the District of Colombia in Washington, D.C.

contentment lit up his visage. He nodded his head in silent approval at my choice of a young madonna-like black woman cradling her sleeping baby in her slender arms. His name, Tyrone, was scratched on the bottom of the sculptured work.

"Fifteen Barbados dollars," he said, "only seven dollars and fifty cents American money."

He gently wrapped the mahogany figurine in a page of the *Advocate News* and took up his preaching again. He warned of the end of the world and the fast approaching Judgment Day. He stopped for a quick smile as we exchanged money and wood carving. As I made my way out of the Gap and onto the main road, his powerful voice followed me, a black Jeremiah shouting at those who would not hear.

I visited the Gap often after the day that I bought the black madonna, but the place under the palm where Tyrone had sat was empty. There was no warning voice to disturb the quiet air and I wondered what had happened to the woodcarving prophet. One evening when I had dinner at the Southern Palms, I asked one of the waiters about Tyrone.

"He crazy, that man!" the waiter explained. "He scare all the tourists away with that hollerin'. The police took him to the Polyclinic where he belong. He better off in the mental hospital."

Almost two years later, as I drove my car past the Southern Palms Hotel, I hit the brakes hard when I saw Tyrone sitting at his old spot under the palm across from the Barclay's Bank. I parked the car, and in my eagerness I almost ran toward the red cloth covered box displaying the carvings. Tyrone did not reply to my greeting. His grey head was sunk down on his chest, and lethargically he chipped away at a small carving. Silent and subdued, he worked at his task. There was not a sound from the former "Old Testament" prophet. The wood carvings were neatly lined up on the red cloth, but they too were silent and devoid of spontaneity. The figure of a woman carrying a basket of dead chickens on her head was repeated again and again. Tyrone and his art were silent, but the wind rustled in the trees and the passing tourists laughed in the tropical sunlight.

Two Weeks in Rosario

Sybil Smith

Rosario is a mountain village in north central Honduras with about three hundred inhabitants. There is no telephone service, no postal service, no power, and, when I went there in 1988, there was no consistent source of clean water. There was a small school, but many of the village children could not go, because they could not afford the required books, pencils, paper, and uniforms. The majority of the inhabitants were farmers, but only a few owned their own land. Most worked for others, as migrant laborers, often rising before dawn and walking hours to reach the place where they would be working.

I went to Rosario with a group called Americans Caring, Teaching and Sharing (ACTS) which was started by a Congregational church in Franconia, New Hampshire. The group's goal was to develop one village at a time, in partnership with the villagers and the Honduran Protestant church, to raise the standard of living of the villagers and the consciousness of the participating Americans. The plan was to send teams to Honduras for two weeks every few months or so. ACTS chose, as its first project, Rosario.

Ms. Smith was born and educated in Vermont, and has traveled widely as a nurse. Her poems have appeared in numerous publications including *New England Review/Bread Loaf Quarterly, Southern Poetry Review, Cumberland Poetry Review, New Virginia Review,* and *Spoon River Quarterly.* Her fiction and non-fiction has appeared in *Spectrum, The Albany Review, Ithaca Womens Anthology, Northern Review, Ellipsis,* and *Vermont Woman.* Fiction is upcoming in an anthology titled *Back in My Body.* She lives in Vermont with her husband and daughter, and works as a psychiatric nurse.

My team was one of the earliest to go. I was asked to participate because I am a nurse, and a friend of the physician who was to lead the expedition. There were six people in the group. Besides the doctor (Dennis) and myself, there were two medical students (Jeff and Kathy), a carpenter (Wade), and an architect (Betsey). Our instructions were to hold a clinic, and to start building the structure that would house the future, and permanent, clinic, and also serve as living quarters for the groups of Americans who would continue to visit. We all paid our own way, which amounted to about $900.00 each. We went in January of 1988.

What follows are my journal entries, woven together with current reflections, in light of who I am: A 35-year old mother, wife, nurse, writer, busywoman; who has not generally involved herself in politics and who half-wishes she could hide in Vermont and let the world go to hell without her feeble attempts at intervention. And who has always half-wished to save the world.

January 16. I have to leave at 4:00 in the morning, and haven't slept well. We've had two days of twenty below weather. You could see the mercury falling hour by hour, and, as my father used to, my husband ambled over to the thermometer periodically to report some new low. He is happy that the house is warm, and the pipes aren't frozen. I am worried about the deer. At 3:30 I sit in our bedroom to say goodbye to my family as they sleep; Celia on her mattress on the floor, and Frank on the bed. I shine my flashlight on Celia's face for one last look at her sweet profile. She is currently afraid of tigers, so she sleeps in our room. I must pretend I am not afraid of tigers, though I am. Of different ones.

At Logan airport. One of our group has just picked up a copy of the *Boston Globe*. In it there is an article about two human rights activists from Honduras—Miguel Pavon and Professor Moises Landa Verde—who were just gunned down in their car in San Pedro Sula, the city where we'll be arriving this afternoon.

At Miami airport. It's as if we're already in a foreign country. The announcements over the intercom are in Spanish. The women in our group seem to be the only ones in the airport not wearing skintight leopard print pants and sequined high heels.

San Pedro Sula airport. There is one landing strip, and it's a short one. My view, as we descend, is of banana groves, so close it seems they must be dusting the bottom of the plane. Then the wheels hit the tarmac, and, surprisingly, everyone in the plane breaks into spontaneous applause. I feel like cheering myself. Wade and I watched what appeared to be jet fuel leaking out of the wing the entire trip.

The airport is a rectangular, cinder block building, which seems quite shabby after the Miami airport. But the air is beautiful; that balmy, fragrant, thick presence that seems to envelop one; especially startling to inhabitants of the northern latitudes. (I lived in Mississippi for a time, and when I left I missed the air most. I had learned, though, that there was a downside to all that warmth and nectar. Things spoiled more quickly. Parasites and scavengers more easily took hold.)

The country from the air looked primeval; a flat, alluvial plain breaking sharply into graceful, green, partly cleared mountains. Down here it is simply low rent: tattered, squalid, and with soldiers primarily on view; only two or three (but startling still), their weapons slung from their shoulders. We have been told not to take their pictures. It is against the law. The soldiers will take your film and fine you if you do.

We stand in line in the airport. In here the air is fetid, like a salt marsh. My chest begins to tighten. I have asthma, and have brought oral prednisone with me in case it acts up. I am thankful that I have this ace in the hole.

The customs official accepts our *"Yo soy tourista. Dos semanas. Hotel Bolivar,"* with a bored, slightly impatient gaze. In this, too, we have been coached. We are not tourists, and we will not be staying at Hotel Bolivar, but this is what we say, to keep it simple. The check of our bags is not exhaustive.

Once we have gone through customs we go outside to look for Joyce, the doctor and missionary who is our liaison in Honduras. She is there, looking as might be expected: plain, middle-aged, pleasant, permanently frazzled. She leads us to her white four-wheel-drive pickup. There is some confusion because five or six men try to take our bags to the car. We are loathe to let go of them, but the men are insistent, so they attach themselves to various odds and ends, some of which we are also holding. At the car they stand around looking expectant, while Joyce looks into her purse indecisively. (Her harried, otherworldly air is her own peculiar adaptation to life in the Third World, and it seems to serve her well.) One small boy is left standing barefoot and tattered in our midst. Kathy leans forward furtively and puts change in his grubby palm.

"You gave him money," says Dennis.

"I know," Kathy replies. (I am on her side. We have been told not to give money but . . .)

"He looks like he could use some," says Joyce, gently, and so the matter is settled. We climb into the truck, and are off to San Pedro Sula. The road is a paved, two-lane highway, but there is another lane, which we start calling "that mystical, magical third lane." Cars and trucks pass whenever the fancy strikes them, responding to some primal urge we do not understand. This means that frequently there are three cars abreast on the highway.

As we approach the city the air quality deteriorates dramatically. Emissions control? No way, José. Smouldering dumps, spewing smokestacks, bus fumes, and open cook fires combine to make a yellowish smog.

I try to take everything in. There are billboards. There is a caterpillar plant. There are banana groves with bunches of bananas swaddled in plastic. There are shanty towns; houses made of scrounged block and tin and wood. Many, many people in the mire and trash are barefoot. I see a little boy peeing into the mud, and have an urge to wash my hands.

Suddenly I realize something. I have become too hygienic. I don't know what it's like anymore to accept it all: mud, offal, grease, spit, snot; human effluvium. It threatens me terribly. I remember an essay I read in *New England Review/Bread Loaf Quarterly*. It was about swimming in the Ganges. There was the image of a woman cleaning her teeth with a twig, dipping it in the water only inches from a floating piece of feces. Corpses released in upstream burials sometimes floated by. It was a relief, the writer said, when he finally walked in, and stood in the filthy, opaque, grungy Ganges. It was a necessary surrender.

And what is the alternative? To be whisked from airport to expensive hotel in an air-conditioned limo, seeing the misery only briefly through a closed window, sneering at the filth and poverty, or, let's be generous, perhaps just turning away with a platitude and a sigh.

January 17. I am already behind in my journal. There is so much to record, I'm overwhelmed.

The night? Pure misery. So tired I couldn't sleep despite two sleeping pills and a beer. Peeing every ten minutes. Coughing and hacking; unable to take a deep breath. I finally got up and took 60 mg of prednisone. I knew that this might keep me wakeful, but there seemed no other way to survive these radical changes of environment, temperature, and mind. Besides, Kathy, Betsey, and I were crammed into one small room, and my coughing and peeing was keeping them awake. The situation was aggravated by the fact that the train was a stone's throw from the hotel, and its whistle blasted us awake at 4:00 A.M. The shower was no consolation. It was one thick, cold rope of water that arced unimpeded from a single pipe in the wall.

But the *café con leche*, coffee with milk, is good, and there's a pretty mezzanine where I now sit writing. The maids are hanging towels all around me on the railing. They have washed them by hand, in tubs. I can't help but see myself through their eyes; a gringa in a peasant dress and sandals, scribbling away. Can they write? What do they think of a woman who, given time and money, chooses to wear shabby clothes and sit around chewing the inside of her cheek, writing as if her life depends on it? The white flags flap all around me. I surrender.

Suddenly I'm happy, headache and all. The adrenal surge is telling me all is well. Good thing too. It's a big day. We go to Joyce's house, which is a pleasant, simple affair in the suburbs. Her adopted Honduran daughter is there, with her baby and the nanny. The TV is always on. The fare is soap operas, and Spanish MTV. We must find Jimmy, who is going to come with us to Rosario. He is our interpreter. Where is Jimmy? He is at church. Where is our car (an Isuzu purchased with ACTS funds)? Juan Alberto has it. Where is Juan Alberto? He is at church too. Who is Juan Alberto? He is someone who works for the Honduran church agency that is our cover. He insists on driving us out to Rosario. Somehow, in a mishmash of English and Spanish and dollars and limpiras and luggage and foodstuff and introductions and good will, we manage to get on our way. We are going in two cars; the Isuzu and the pickup. The seat belts have been ripped out of (or never came in) the pickup, but the Isuzu still has them. Thank God for small favors. I am in the Isuzu with Betsey and Kathy. Juan Alberto, who speaks no

English, is driving. I sit up front, with my harness secure. Mario Andretti, eat your heart out.

I took Spanish in high school, and French in college. I keep speaking French instead of Spanish, but Juan Alberto takes it all in stride, and bit by bit, my Spanish improves. I keep leaning close to him, as if to absorb his meaning by sheer proximity. He is expansive. I believe he is pointing out landmarks that he thinks Americans will like: plantations, electric power plants, military installations.

We stop for lunch on the main highway. We have soda in green glass bottles, rice, beans, tortillas, cole slaw, and soup. Kathy has a chicken claw floating in her soup. I can't touch mine, so I give it to Jimmy. He is young, and very skinny.

After lunch, we leave the highway and begin the climb into the mountains. It is cleaner—prettier. Juan Alberto begins to stop when he sees pedestrians, and they hop into the back with a grin and rapid-fire Spanish. Soon we are crammed full. This is the etiquette of the road. If you have room, you pick people up.

Finally, we turn onto a winding dirt road. This is the road to Rosario. It is what we call class four in Vermont. In other words, you better have four-wheel-drive, and plenty of nerve. We jolt over miles of washouts and potholes, past forest and ravine, till we come out, quite suddenly, into the village. The shouts of people and barking of dogs rise around us, but we don't stop. We drive on to the area where we are to pitch our tents. I am amazed to see that, surrounding our "compound" (a brambly lot enclosed by barbed wire fence) are daub and wattle huts. The pigs, chickens, cows, and horses are loose. There is dust and manure and smoke and noise galore. The scene is positively medieval.

I smile a lot, and let the others take over. Joyce and Jimmy ease the transition. We unload the trucks, while the village men begin hacking at the brambles in our camp site with machetes. Suddenly we notice that our ankles are stinging. We look down and see small ants swarming over our shoes. But of course. Next thing you know it will be gnats, or leeches.

My journal gets thin here. As near as I can recall we set up the tents, and went to Sonia's house in the upper village. The upper village was a lot better off than the lower village. The houses were made of adobe instead of sticks and mud. Sonia and her mother had been hired to cook our meals and do our wash. We ate supper at her house, in an area that was roofed, but otherwise open. We had forgotten our lanterns, and it was very dark, so after supper I offered to drive to the tents and get them so we could stay up and talk a bit. Wade said he'd come with me, but he didn't want to drive. Once on the road I realized that I was high as a kite, from a weird combination of fatigue and prednisone. I negotiated the streams and potholes with aplomb, while Wade looked at me with amazement. "Where the hell are you from?" he said.

January 18. Our first full day in Rosario. We are waked at first light by the crowing of roosters, the barking of dogs, the lowing of cattle, the grunting of pigs, and the shouts of men taking their herds of horses and cows out to pasture in the hills. The animals shamble by on both sides of our compound. We crawl out of our tents, brush our teeth with our precious bottles of *aqua purificada*, purified water, and try to find somewhere to pee. We have no latrine of our own yet, and the barbed wire of our compound is ringed by giggling groups of children, who are fascinated by our every move. Finally we walk some distance, and use a villager's latrine. The latrines here are nothing but a cement ring, with no seat, so one has to perch on or slightly above the cold, dirty, wet cement lip, meanwhile trying not to breathe and not to touch anything. Then, of course, there is no running water. At one time a system of pipes was set up in the village, fed by a holding tank in the hills, but it was poorly designed, never worked well, and finally broke down almost entirely, except for a few spigots in the upper village, which work for a few hours a day. Sonia has a spigot that sometimes works. In the meantime we make do with wet naps. I always have a large supply of these premoistened towelettes in my pockets.

We walk up to Sonia's for breakfast. During breakfast we plan our strategy for the day. Betsey and Wade will help the men set up tent platforms, and start building a latrine, and Dennis, Jeff, Kathy, Joyce, and I will see patients. We are to use Renee's house as the temporary clinic. Renee is the president of the village communal, and is also Sonia's brother. His house is right across from hers. He is . . . how can I say . . . words fail me. Quite the dude. He sends frissons of illicit feeling up and down my spine, and me a married lady. He is bigger than most of the village men, very well-built, and still quite young. He may be twenty-six or twenty-seven. He has movie-star good looks, dresses nicely, and wears a cowboy hat. He is somewhat aloof from all the excitement over the Americans, though he is quite insistent that we use his house for clinic. He moves into the tiny kitchen with his present lady friend, a plump, giggly young woman named Alba, who attends to his every need. He spends a lot of time outside his house, talking on the porch, watching the patients assemble. For me and the other American women he has a polite but penetrating stare.

The trickle of patients is slow at first. It takes time for the word to get around that the Americans are in town. Also, Rosario is fairly remote, so people cannot come by bus, but must walk or ride burros. The lucky ones catch a ride in beat-up trucks. The patients do not speak English. We do not speak Spanish. The first day Joyce is with us, and things go smoothly. But how will we fare when she is gone? We will have to depend on Jimmy.

What do the patients have? Infections. Parasites. Colds. Coughs. Skin irritations. And headaches, backaches, bodyaches, toothaches, stomachaches. No wonder. They work hard, all the time. They drink coffee the color and consistency of hot tar. They are exposed to constant dust, animal hair, and smoke. They drink water that is not clean by our standards. They live in houses without screens, or glass windows, for that matter. They have very little access to dental or eye care. One of the big attractions is our box full of American eyeglasses. No matter that they may not be exactly the right prescription! The patients rummage; try each one on. When they arrive at a pair that seems to help, they are happy. No matter that they may not be a flattering frame! I saw an old man walk away with a pair of cat's eye glasses. I saw a young woman pick black-framed, squarish, men's glasses. Vanity pales beside the ability to finally sew, or read, or *see*.

Since there are many of us at the clinic, we take turns slipping off in pairs, and walk up the road to a certain bathing spot. We wash in the trickle of a small waterfall, in sight of the road. The area is muddy, and not as idyllic as it may sound.

At the end of the day, it's supper at Sonia's again, then bed as soon as it gets dark. I sleep well, despite the discomfort, the prednisone, the culture shock.

January 19. This morning we tour Mauricio's kitchen garden. Mauricio is Sonia's father, and she lives with him. The house where we eat is home to Mauricio, Julia (his wife, Sonia's mother), Sonia, and three of Sonia's four children. Sonia's husband, she tells us, is "wet back" (her term) in Miami.

Mauricio is a wiry, friendly, hardworking man. In his garden he has corn, beans, oranges, lemons, guavas, tomato seedlings, oregano, and cocoa. Jimmy tells us they also grow marijuana. Mauricio is well-off, comparatively. He owns a good chunk of land outside the village, on the road that goes by our tent and farther into the mountains.

Now that Joyce is gone I am getting to know Jimmy quite well. He is in his early twenties, and teaches English in San Pedro. He was adopted by American missionaries when he was seven days old, and he grew up in their home. His American mother had diabetes, though, and was forced by illness to return to the States when Jimmy was sixteen. They got one Honduran son back with them, but Jimmy wasn't able to get a visa, so he had to stay. Joyce became his unofficial mother. This, at any rate, is what Jimmy says.

Strategy for the day? It is decided that since the clinic is not all that busy yet, Dennis, Jeff, Betsey, and Kathy will take trips to the remote villages in the hills, some of which can be reached only on foot or burro. I will stay back at the clinic, with Jimmy. This seems to work okay. I have been a nurse practitioner, and so am used to diagnosis and treatment. If I think someone needs to see Dennis, I tell them to wait for him to return.

January 20. We are glad that the latrine is being made. Some among us have diarrhea. I won't go into the nitty-gritty—suffice to imagine having to answer an urgent call of nature in the middle of the night, in a sleeping village, in a tent compound with no latrine, and no running water, in a region where reputedly there are large snakes. Like cats in cat litter some of us have taken to digging holes in the dirt that has been dug from the latrine hole, and is heaped in a mound in back of the tents.

Today I go with Jeff to Yoro, to buy nails and cement. Yoro is a biggish city to the east of Rosario. On the way, on a long straight stretch of paved highway, I notice several dead horses and cows, bloating in the sun. They appear to have been hit by cars. We decide to stop at the hospital in Yoro, to say hello and to drop off some donated supplies. We have been told by previous groups that the hospital is free, but that it seldom has medicine. This has been confirmed by the people coming to our clinic, who—by the way—pay for the medication we dispense.

The hospital is another of your basic cinder block rectangles. The doctor, who seems amused by us, offers a tour. I try not to let my horror show as we are led through the wards. There are few nurses to be seen. There are flies everywhere, and some of the sick barely have enough energy to brush them away. They lie listlessly in crowded ward rooms, with dirty dressings and open sores. We see a woman in labor, and one with a brand new baby. The doctor asks me if I want to assist with a delivery. "I am dirty," I say. "Here it doesn't matter," he replies. Of the fifty or so people we see (malnutrition, diabetes, ulcers, abscesses) three are victims of machete fights. One is a woman, whose husband has chopped off her right arm. Her face is slashed down its entire length, and her head is wrapped in a bloody turban.

After leaving the hospital, we go into the center of the city. It looks like a town in the old American Southwest; dusty unpaved streets lined by one story buildings, and open markets. I buy rubber thongs (*chiclettas*, the villagers call them). We see an American army jeep, in which loll two big (do Americans look big!) men, who look like they stepped from the pages of *Soldier of Fortune*. As we leave the city we see another jeep, and two more American soldiers. Then, when we turn onto the highway, Jimmy points down a new dirt road. "There is a *contra* base," he says. I ask Jimmy what he thinks of the *contra* situation. "It's like this," he says, in his adequate but stilted English. "They are here for money. If we will not let them be here, we will not get the American money. They are run by the rich people who used to own everything in Nicaragua."

In the afternoon, after I get back from Yoro, I work in the clinic for awhile. I see a woman named Eleanor, a fifty-eight-year old who looks seventy, who is missing one eye, and nearly blind in the other. Her complaints are numerous, and are probably all true. After she is seen, she sits on the clinic steps, and will not go. She mutters on and on in a sorrowing voice about her pain, about her terrible life. The other villagers humor her at first; then seem to grow embarrassed. They begin to kid her. Jimmy says that she is insisting that we take her to the United States. The villagers are telling her she shouldn't go to the

States, because when you are bad there they make you into candles and paper! Finally someone gets Julia, and she gently leads Eleanor away.

January 21. Eleanor comes to Sonia's in the morning, and sits at the breakfast table. She talks nonstop in Spanish, although we do our best to ignore her. We continue to talk about our upcoming day. I whisper to Jimmy, "Does she know no one is listening?" Suddenly Jimmy jumps up, practically apoplectic with laughter. He is doubled over, choking. Finally he tells us that Eleanor is asking us to implant an English-speaking tape recorder in her brain, so that she can come to the United States with us.

The clinic is very busy today. The word has gotten out. We see a little boy with a cellulitis of the face and jaw, from an abscessed lymph node. He is listless and dehydrated. We give him a huge shot of antibiotics, and tell the mother she must come back the next day. This is a child who would probably have died if we had not been there.

January 22. Today is Friday, and we're going to spend the weekend at Puerto Cortes, in a resort hotel. We need a little R&R. This morning though, we see the sick, flooding in. The little boy is back, slightly better, and we give him another shot. We see a woman with PID [pelvic inflammatory disease], from a poorly performed tubal ligation. We see a woman with a tooth so badly abscessed that there is a drainage point on the skin of her jaw. We see a boy with an unhealed compound fracture of the leg. He has osteomyelitis. The leg should be amputated.

I had an interesting exchange with Renee this morning. There is a picture of him tacked to the wall of the room in which we're holding clinic. It shows him in a macho squat, in army uniform, holding a gun. I want to learn more about him, so I admire the picture, and ask how he liked being in the army. He says he liked it okay, but would rather be in Rosario. Then he says there is an American from ACTS who might come to live in Rosario. The American, Jack, is a special friend of his. Jack likes politics, he adds. "Many of us are interested in politics," I say, "but we are careful not to stick our noses where they don't belong." Jimmy translates. Renee laughs.

After lunch, we pile into the Isuzu, and head for San Pedro. We will visit Joyce before we go to Puerto Cortes. On the trip it starts to rain. Looking into the barrios from the car, I see how miserable life would be there during rainy season. The yards are a miasma of tin cans, trash, old shoes, glass, tires, and feces. The water sits in pools on the soaked ground. The children are barefoot, and don't seem to have warm clothes. How does anyone survive it?

January 23–24. We stay at the Hotel Playa. There is hot water. It rains or is overcast all weekend, and we do little except read, wash, eat, and rest. Our only *tourista* act is to visit a huge, magical, architecturally astounding Spanish fort.

January 25. The rain seems to have brought cold with it. I am not prepared for chilly weather. I am wearing an eccentric outfit —silk long johns and a turtleneck under an Indonesian cotton dress, topped with a flannel chamois shirt. Oh, *and* knee socks with clunky leather shoes.

I feel quite adjusted to life in Rosario. I know exactly what to carry with me now, and how to dress. My little corner of the tent is organized just so.

I have begun to get to know the little girls who constantly press around me. Some hang back at the barbed wire, but some stand inches away, and finger my belongings. Today I notice a shy girl in a filthy black dress. She seems more neglected than the others. I beckon for her to come to me, and tell her to sit down. Suddenly I'm inspired to comb her hair, which is spiked and matted. She has lice. Jimmy comes over to translate for me. I tell her to come to the clinic for lice medicine. Her father went away to the city, and doesn't live with them. Her father doesn't love her. Her mother had nine children. Six are dead. She, Marta, is the only girl alive. When I am done with her hair I put it in a pony tail. Then I get wet wipes and clean her face and hands. I get out my mirror, but she turns away. She won't look at herself.

Today the clinic is busy. Renee has put new cement on his steps, and is making adobes for the future clinic. Our latrine is finished, but the cement seat must harden, so we still can't use it. Betsey and Kathy have made a study of the old water system. They think it can be fixed, but it will take money, and expertise.

January 26. Again this morning Marta comes to see me. She is the only one to appear. The cold must be keeping the others in.

She crouches in the lee of our tents, with her knees up inside her thin dress, pressed against her chest. I want to give her one of my blankets, but I know the others wouldn't like it. (We have been told not to give anything away, since that promotes a begging mentality.) She looks so cold that finally I ask her to come sit beside me, and I wrap my arm around her. She sinks into me, and soon puts her head in my lap. The others are getting ready to go to Yoro, because Dennis wants to see the hospital. I am angry at them. I think that when they leave, I will give Marta a blanket. I feel like crying. I try with all my will not to, but it's no use. Marta doesn't notice at first, but then she feels me shaking. She twists her face around and stares up into my face. She looks confused. Has she done something wrong? What does the fat gringa have to cry about? *"Esta bien,"* I tell her. *"Esta bien."* Of course, it's not okay. She is cold, wet, and hungry, and has lice. If someone (God, the president, *someone*), came up to me right now and said, "She's yours, you can take her home with you," I would do so without a moment's hesitation. (If someone were to call me now, and tell me she was waiting at the airport, I would get into my car and drive there as fast as I could. That is how I feel about Marta.)

January 27. Marta comes again this morning. Last night I lay awake and conceived of a plan. I would take her up to the waterfall, with my soap, my shampoo, some Kwell, and the rubber bands that Jeff bought me in Yoro. I would bathe her whole body carefully, wash her dress, and braid her hair. But today I see it is too cold to bathe. Instead I wrap a blanket around us, and we snuggle. Some others girls join us, until there are four of us in a row.

Work on the new clinic has stopped, because of the cold and rain. We have decided to leave tomorrow, instead of Friday.

After seeing patients we prepare a piñata for the children. Jimmy bought it. He puts candy in it, and we add rubberbands, pens, pencils, earrings, and other odds and ends. We hang the piñata from a tree, and a great crowd gathers. It is festive.

Since it is our last evening, a crowd comes to our tents in the evening. They are all dressed up, and some are carrying tape decks. They have brought us an orange cake, baked in Sonia's beehive oven. There is also orange soda. Though it's raining we stand around eating and listening to music. One villager has brought some American music. (I remember one particular song; it was "Love Hurts.")

Several villagers give speeches of gratitude. Dennis and I also give brief speeches, but I can't remember mine. Everything is getting pretty blurry by this point, and I am soon to find out why. I go to bed, and notice that I am feeling slightly nauseated, so I put a garbage bag by my head. It's a good thing. I wake at midnight and vomit so quickly that I barely have time to get my head in the bag. Kathy wakes up. "Whoa," she says, and, despite the fact that I feel totally miserable, this provokes a fit of giggling. I lie in bed the rest of the night shivering and vomiting. Kathy begins to feel sick too. In the morning I begin having diarrhea, and I'm not able to go to breakfast. Marta comes to the tent, but I can't get up and sit with her. I'm too miserable. I try to explain as I stumble by to the latrine that I'm sick, but she doesn't seem to understand. She scuffles around outside on the tent platform, and I can hear her talking to me. *"Tiene frio gringa?"* she asks. Are you cold?

The others come back from breakfast, and break down the tents. I lie in the back of the Isuzu, rising only to go to the latrine. As a result, I barely remember saying goodbye. I do remember one thing, though. I gave Marta a blanket.

January 29. I have missed Celia and Frank terribly. I brought a picture of them to Honduras, and every day I took it out and looked at it. I have not been able to call, since phone service is very poor in Honduras. One can only call from a central international line in San Pedro Sula, and there is always a huge wait.

As soon as I get to the Miami airport, I call Celia. She is at my sister's house. When I hear her voice, I start to cry, and can't say much except, "I'm coming home, honey. I missed you." She is very mature about it. "Don't cry, Mommy," she tells me.

I am ten pounds lighter, and my skin is a few shades darker. I look like I've been to a health spa, and, in a way, I have—the Bleeding Heart Health Spa, Rosario, Honduras. Sometimes I have felt cynical about this whole project. I've speculated that it's just a way for doctors and architects and lawyers with liberal leanings to think they've "done something." "Oh yes," they can say, "I went to Honduras, and worked in a little village there." "Oh how wonderful," their friends will reply, "would you like another hors d'oeuvre?"

But, more often, I have felt that ACTS is on the right track. Perhaps it's true that some of the Americans who go will treat the trip as a novelty, an experience that serves to make their comfort yet more comfortable. But certainly for others it will be the first door they open into a new way of thinking and living. These brave ones aren't sure what is behind the door, but they open it.

This, I think, is the way to grow. Don't expect to start with answers. Don't expect your quest to be perfectly pure. Just start walking, and keep a modicum of faith that you will stumble along with good intentions, and an open mind.

Besides, as I sit here writing, two years later, certain things are undeniably different. There is a clinic building in Rosario now. The water system has been fixed, and all the spigots work. Sonia saved enough money, working for Americans, to illegally join her husband in Miami. The boy with the infected fracture of his leg was flown to the States, and had complicated surgery. The leg was saved. Marta is still alive. She looks okay, they tell me.

Bocaraca

Michael Johnson

W hen the two forest guards invited me to go with them to Corcovado National Park, I didn't hesitate. We left before daybreak and arrived at a farmer's house in time to eat a corn tortilla and drink coffee for breakfast.

The trail was good, not muddy as it is in summertime, and it wasn't too steep for the horses. By the time we reached a clearing at the top of the mountains it was becoming quite warm, but it was cool again once we submerged ourselves beneath the protective rain forest canopy. The trail wasn't too bad for the descent, either. It became necessary to separate widely at one point where it was extremely steep and narrow with no extra room. Carlos, who has the best eyes and the most experience, was our leader. I followed and the other forest guard brought up the rear.

Suddenly Carlos' horse leaped forward as he pointed at a low, overhanging branch, shouting *"Culebra! Culebra!"* Snake! I looked closely where he pointed and eventually made out the well-camouflaged, green and yellow, two-and-a-half-foot *bocaraca* coiled around the branches. The *bocaraca* is a venomous, arboreal

---

Armed with a degree in agriculture from Montana State University, Mr. Johnson set out for hard work and adventure to the tropical moist forests of Costa Rica, where he not only encountered venomous snakes, friendly people, animals, and plants that glow in the dark, but romance as well. He worked for two years in that wonderful land as a forestry extensionist. He is now employed as a schoolteacher in Denver and bores his class every year with his slides of Central America. He'll never forget coming back to the United States, going to the supermarket, and the cashier asking him matter-of-factly, "Paper or plastic?" His reply? "Paper or plastic WHAT?"

snake with a neatly shaped, triangular head that appears much too large for its body. With his sharp eyes, Carlos cheated death by seeing it and dodging to the side just moments before brushing by. The branch the bocaraca was in hung so low the snake would have struck him in the face.

I took a machete from the guard behind me and drew as close as I dared to the snake, striking it with a downward swipe. The blow merely made the demon mad, for it cut off four inches of the tail and knocked it so it hung even lower from the tree. It now hung so low it was impossible for any rider to go by without drawing within striking distance.

It was a terrible demon, staring at me with hate filled eyes, its mouth wide open, fangs flickering out, beckoning me, waiting for the moment when I would draw close enough for it to strike. That moment came when my horse, a stallion who gets impatient if he stands in one spot too long, decided to resume the journey and continued walking downhill. There was no way out. The snake hung so precipitously low I couldn't stoop low enough in the saddle for it not to hit me. I did not have time to jump out of the saddle and there was no side room as the trail was eighteen inches wide at this point.

I pulled back hard on the reins and got Bubba, my horse, to stop directly underneath the snake. I leaned back in the saddle as far as I could, staring at the opened "jaws of hell." I was afraid to take another swipe at my adversary for fear of injury to my horse, as the snake hung directly above Bubba's neck. As I strained against the reins, my eyes opened as big as saucers, leaning as far back as I could go, the two forest guards took the only sensible course of action available to them. They laughed. Seeing no recourse, I took a chance and slashed at the monster, adding years to my life when its head flew into the bush.

All Jerson Needed Was a Chance

Ed and Mary Warmoth

If someone asked you to state your "most rewarding experience" as a U.S. Peace Corps volunteer, what would it be?

We face that question frequently. For us, it was working with Jerson, a young boy who lives in the rural community of Matayaya, across the street from the house we called our Peace Corps home. Jerson is special for many reasons. He's mentally retarded from brain damage caused by high fever meningitis when he was two years old. It was a thrill to have a birthday party for his eighth birthday, and realize how far Jerson had come since we first saw him crawling on the floor and being treated like an animal.

Our friendship with Jerson dates back to August 1985, our first month in Matayaya. We had met other members of the family, ten in all, and went to their house to have lunch. Jerson was on the floor without a stitch of clothes and with a furious look on his face. We were advised that he was loco and not to pay any attention to him.

We began to make contact with Jerson. It's hard to remember the first day he came to our house, but November 30 is written in our diary as the day he learned to pick up a crayon and color. Likely it was also the first day he had seen a crayon. We always had a good supply of crayons, coloring books, and reading

---

Ed and Mary Warmoth were "older American" Peace Corps volunteers from May 1985 to May 1987 in the Dominican Republic following Ed's retirement in 1985 from a public administration career. They have now returned to their home in Oregon, west of Portland, and continue to do volunteer duty, taking assignments with Habitat for Humanity International.

books thanks to cooperative friends in the United States. Like good grandparents, we kept a sack of blocks—salvaged from a furniture shop—and Jerson learned to ask for them and stack one on another.

As the weeks passed we placed trust in Jerson, letting him carry cups from the table, sending him on errands to his house, and letting him participate in the work we were doing in the garden or around the house. He came daily to our gate and called for us by name. It was a while before he could respond with his own name, and still may tell you "yo."

A really big step came in November 1986 when Bea Cravatta, a Peace Corps volunteer with special education training, came in response to our invitation and interviewed Jerson and his mother. She classified his level as "trainable," according to United States standards, and estimated his maximum level might be that of a nine-year old, mentally.

Bea recommended coaching and training procedures to deal with his bad conduct, times when he refused to leave the house or would become upset for some reason. Checking his medication was another suggestion from Bea when she learned he was on phenobarbital morning and night. Many times Jerson would seem to drop off to sleep very suddenly although he was normally playful and energetic.

We took Jerson and his mother to see a special doctor in San Juan and wound up with a recommendation to contact the Dominican Centro de Rehabilitación. Our preliminary visit to the office in Santo Domingo bounced us back to the field office in San Juan. Several phone calls later we were back for a standard limb and coordination check, but with an appointment referral to a neurologist in Santo Domingo.

Back in the *campo*, the country, Jerson is learning new concepts all the time. Frequently he'll point at something and ask the name. He has his favorite books with animal pictures and can recognize them by the cover. His family is amazed at the things he knows and can do.

We gave him a chance to show that he is a human being, and he came through with flying colors. Hopefully his family and the community will fill the gap now that we have moved on.

Cuernavaca

Joanne Rains

I remember an event involving our clinic and a weathered mother who walked uncounted miles with an ill infant. A doctor from Cuernavaca staffed the clinic; we assisted with treatments, finding medicines, and doing health teaching. This gravely ill infant needed an antibiotic and the doctor asked that I find a vial. We were out. I scanned the shelves through donated bottles of tranquilizers and sleep aids, which spoke of American culture and not the needs of developing rural Mexico. When I could not find any antibiotic, I offered to walk with the mother to another clinic site, about a mile away, in hopes that the needed remedy would be found. Without a moment's complaint, she walked with the limp infant in her arms. In the other clinic, the antibiotics were also gone. I was completely devastated, for it was my clinical conclusion that the infant would die without it. How could I tell her? When I explained there was no medicine, she calmly and graciously thanked me for looking, and turned to begin the long walk home. I sat and wept as I watched her figure follow the winding path into the rural hills, and I marveled at her acceptance and calm. My vision of what is "adequate" or "plenty" has never been the same.

Dr. Rains recently completed her doctorate in "Health Policy and Health of the Community" from Indiana University. She is involved in a research project called "Healthy Cities Indiana," which is funded by the W. K. Kellogg Foundation.

Passages

Krystyna Lloyd

At home, above my writing table, I have hung a shawl that a Guatemalan friend sold to me. Sometimes I think I can still smell her sweat when I take it down and wrap it around my shoulders. Years ago I stood in her dusty courtyard and watched her weave on a backstrap loom. Her son was strapped onto her back in a *cargador*, a large handwoven shawl, and a five-year old daughter practiced on a small clumsy loom beside her. The shawl is a smooth and soft cotton, and the colors and design evoke the mystery of another country, another century.

Under the desk is a box of assorted family photographs. Buried under the newer glossier pictures are a few old black-and-white photographs of my Guatemalan life. They are ten years old and starting to crack and curl at the edges, but the faces have not lost their sharpness, nor have I lost the depth of emotion I feel when I look at them. I hold them now, searching for an image that can help me resolve past and present lives without harsh judgments.

Photo No. 1. Surrounded by a group of women and children who have come from the neighboring town of San Andreas Itzapa, I stand with my husband and a fellow relief worker listening to their various health problems. Most mornings there

Krys Lloyd is an artist and writer and lives in Massachusetts with her husband and three teenagers. She also works as a freelance art critic and hopes to continue weaving visual and literary images together, communicating, and sharing with more and more people. She was born in a Polish refugee camp in England in 1949, and has lived in the United States for the past thirty years (except for the year in Guatemala).

would be such a group of women and children outside of our tent door waiting to talk to us. Standing behind me is a silver-haired woman whose sputum I checked in our laboratory for tuberculosis. Because my father died of tuberculosis I was more susceptible to developing the disease. I repeated the tests over and over (the procedure was difficult and problematic) as if through her cure I would somehow gain a sense of victory over a power that took my father away from me when I was a child of seven.

Photo No 2. Daughter in lap, I am sitting on the sunny deck of a tent platform. We slept better under canvas in earthquake country. El Fuego, a live volcano, exhaled smoke and dust over the eastern horizon. Small tremors were part of our daily life. We felt better when the water in our glasses shook to the earth's trembling. Then we would know that there was no huge anger building up in the ground under our beds.

Our encampment was located in the highlands of central Guatemala, an area called the "land of eternal spring" because of the moderate climate and lush vegetation. We were about eighteen adults and ten children, most from the United States, but funded by the Canadian government.

Our tents were erected in a semicircle and faced the crumbling remains of a coffee plantation villa. The owner lived in a larger house in San Andreas Itzapa. We were easy renters. A well cleaner started up the old well for us, and a central kitchen was erected on the tiled floor of the former porch of the villa. Settled homesteaders, we watched the coffee beans grow around us. My family's tent stood underneath an old avocado tree, the fruit of which fell, as it ripened, onto the canvas roof of our tent. In this photo, sitting under the tree, is Verhinja (the Spanish pronunciation of Virginia) who was the first woman to come to us for help with childbirth. The sunlight in the picture warms me even now.

The chicken that made it possible to deliver the baby of this Mayan woman is not in the picture, but I remember it well. Were it not for its presence in the camp, we would never have delivered any babies in these highlands.

An experienced midwife had come with us to the Guatemalan highlands to both deliver babies and help train the local midwives. Several Indian midwives came to our meetings and we tried to explain simple but important methods, such as washing hands before reaching for the baby's head as it presents itself. Our attempts were sometimes too long of a reach across the century of science that lay between us—our description of germs probably sounded as wild to them as their superstitions did to us. For the first six months no native woman came to us to deliver her baby although the Indian women came to us for help when their children were sick. For reasons unknown to us, they only smiled and nodded when we offered our help, at no charge, in childbirth.

One day a chicken appeared in our camp—an escapee from someone's dinner. The chicken decided our encampment was home and we decided our site would be a refuge for the chicken. The native Indians just could not understand why we did not eat this tasty strutting meal. We tried to explain we were vegetarians, but it was beyond their comprehension that anyone could pass up a meal for such a strange-sounding principle. They were probably too hungry to understand.

The chicken had been scratching among our tents for a few months when Verhinja arrived, in labor, at the camp. Debra, who was the most fluent in Spanish and often helped Carolyn, the midwife, set up her tent for the delivery. I was asked to assist. I was to suction, clean, and care for the newborn baby.

This was Verhinja's third baby and her labor intensified when she laid down, after having walked three miles from her home. We tried to convince her husband to stay in the room, but he said he could not bear to listen to her groans. After she had pushed out a baby girl, I cut the umbilical cord and suctioned a slippery newborn as she breathed her first fresh air. The beauty of the birth filled me with the same wonder and joy I had felt at the birth of my own children. I cradled a perfect child in my arms. Verhinja smiled at us and for an instant we shared a mutual motherhood I had never felt before.

When I had finished clothing the baby, I held her out to her own mother, but Verhinja turned her back to me, too tired to take yet another burden into her already harsh life. Juan came back in and smiled at his daughter, looking pleased, almost as if he had won a bet. "You have taken good care of my wife and baby. It is good we came here. There was talk in the town that you had come here to eat Guatemalan babies—that was why you would deliver for no money. But I saw that you did not eat the chicken and so I did not believe this talk." A local midwife, afraid of losing business, probably helped spread the rumor, but I understood a little more how strange we must have looked to these townspeople.

It soon became obvious to the women of the town that we did not eat babies, and many came to us for help with pregnancy and labor. I know why I look so tired in the first photograph. It was a hard life to love these people. There was so much to give—just knowing a few simple medical facts could save a life—yet the people's trust was so hard to win.

Photo No. 3. A picture of the new clinic, built of wood instead of adobe, brings back a harsher memory. The wood had been shipped all the way from Canada, and the building looked alien in a town of cane and adobe homes. Yet we all felt safer under wood. The tile-roofed, large adobe buildings seemed ominous in a land of earthquakes.

My husband and I had set up a medical laboratory in the local town clinic soon after arriving in Guatemala. After a month of working in San Andreas he was more determined than ever to become a medical doctor. Already on a waiting list of applicants at the University of Massachusetts School of Medicine in Amherst, but unsure of the status of his application, he enrolled in the University of Guatemala in Guatemala City. This meant daily classes for him, and I took over all of the lab work in the clinic.

Our two children, a three-year old boy and a one-year old girl, were taken care of by friends at our encampment. Our daughter, Katie, cried constantly because she was not used to the longer hours I needed in order to take care of what both my husband and I had done together before.

I tried to keep Katie out of my mind as I worked during the quiet lunch hour of one very memorable day. Slides had to be prepared and stains fixed as I tried to determine which parasite was flourishing in a child I had seen that morning—the same size as Katie, but three years older. Too often I heard church bells toll for tiny coffins. Though the clinic was closed for lunch, there was a knock on the door. I pulled myself away from the microscope reluctantly, hoping it was not an emergency, and answered the door.

An unusual sight greeted me—two Americans—what appeared to be overweight *touristas,* tourists. These were the first Americans I had seen in the seven months I had been in the Guatemalan highlands, other than fellow relief workers.

"Hello," I said, impatient to get back to my work, "we are closed right now, but what do you need?" A look of relief and smiles flooded their faces. "Oh! You speak English. How wonderful. We are looking for a fountain we saw in our guidebook. Could you tell us where it is?"

They opened a tourist guidebook and showed me the name of a fountain they could not pronounce. They were so happy to have found an American, but to me they looked alien. I felt repulsed by what I perceived to be their blindness to what was around them. It seemed they had come to see only what was in their travel agency brochure and were missing the people, the reality of what was before them. I wanted to tell them enough of what we were doing in Guatemala to ask for a much needed contribution, but my pride and self-righteousness overcame me.

"Your guidebook is old—there was an earthquake here last year and I know of no such fountain. You should stay in Guatemala City if you want to use guidebooks." Angrily I thought of Theresa, whose malnourished twin baby, Elmar, I had seen in the clinic yesterday. Theresa had told me she worked in a large tourist hotel where she was paid a dollar for a day's work. Rudely, I closed the door in their faces, catching a look of astonishment on the woman's face as I narrowly missed her fingers.

The solid wooden door closed. I was alone once again in the clinic. In a vivid flash I saw my American parents' faces imposed over the faces of those tourists walking away from the clinic. I was in Guatemala because I had rejected their values. Yet adopting values that were opposite to theirs had not let me escape who I still was. That was, too recognizably, not Guatemalan. Suddenly I knew, with a foreboding certainty, that I would be leaving Guatemala soon. I knew that I would have to find a way to live, a way to sleep at night, and a way to wake up in the morning in the United States of America.

That evening, in a message from Massachusetts that had to be relayed through California on our short wave radio, Gregg and I found out that he had been accepted to medical school in Amherst. The radio band was dropping out as the sun set and we had to shout over and over, "We accept. We accept." This was late spring and he was to start in the fall. We left a month later toward an old but strange reality.

An Old Story

Marnie Mueller

"I'll remind you, Caitlin, I'm not a novice at organizing. I worked in Chicago with Saul Alinsky for many years. I'm well aware of what can and can't be done."

"I know all about that," I said, trying to control my voice in the Peace Corps office where we sat. I'd heard the director's Saul Alinsky line at least once a week in the six months he'd been in-country. "But this is my neighborhood. I've lived there a year and a half. I know what'll happen."

"Caitlin, you're overexcited. You've blown this out of proportion."

Bob Stevens, a little man with a blond crew cut, sat as he always did with his stubby legs up on his desk and chomped on his cigar. On the wall in front of him was a strategy map of Guayaquil with pins of various colors stuck in all the barrios where volunteers were stationed. My blue pin jabbed the Cerro Santa Ana, a hill on the north side of the city. It was where I not only lived, but worked as an organizer. I wasn't a novice either, I wanted to tell him. I knew all about self-determination and ferreting out needs and spotting leadership, but most of all, I knew about not raising expectations too high.

"The navy and the consulate want proof for the stateside businesses that made the donations. Understandably," he said,

Marnie Mueller was a volunteer with one of the first Peace Corps groups working in Ecuador, South America, from 1963 to 1965. She is just finishing a novel partially based on her experience there. Her poetry and short stories have been published widely, most recently in *Village Voice Literary Supplement* and *Home to Stay: Asian American Fiction by Women*, published by Greenfield Press.

glancing sideways at me. He began to rock back and forth in his chair, pushing off the desk with his feet. Outside the noon sun blasted straight down, stifling all sound and movement. A floor fan by the window whirred heavy hot air toward me. The short-wave radio squawked. "They want to bring the goods in and make a presentation."

"What do you mean, presentation?"

"They'll come in with their truck. You have your *presidente* there. Some of the people from the barrio. Some kids. *Niños.* From your school program. We'll give the kids dolls, the women fabric, and take a picture."

"I've worked a year and a half convincing people that I didn't come here to bring manna from heaven," I said. I was trembling, recalling how during my first six months in the neighborhood my one goal had been to stop people from begging from me. "Please," they would whine, inclining their heads. "Be a good gringa. Give me a little gift. You are rich." It was only after we got beyond that that we began to get any real work done.

"They finally believe me. They've worked their tails off to make a go of their own community center. If you bring in all that merchandise at once you'll destroy everything I've tried to do. Please, let me integrate it slowly into the programs. I'll take photos each time. I promise."

"I'll take it under consideration," he said without looking at me.

"If you bring that stuff into my neighborhood, you'll start a riot."

"I think we're finished, aren't we?"

"You can't come in, I'm warning you."

He dropped his feet, bent over the desk, and began looking through his papers. "If we decide to do it, I assure you that it will be done with care. Intelligently."

I walked across the plaza toward the hill. Where some days I wished for nothing more than to be away from the noise and poverty of the barrio, that afternoon, following my argument with Bob Stevens, it looked beautiful to me. The wide cement stairs that rose steeply from the street were laced with people—vendors balancing wooden trays loaded with produce on their heads; women returning from their husband's work with the three-tiered lunch pails that had earlier been filled with soup, rice, and salad; neighbors standing around in postsiesta conversation. Two- and three-story cane houses lined the stairs on either side, their pastel pinks and yellows and turquoises bleached to a chalky softness in the harsh, early afternoon sun. Even the river Guayas that flowed by slow and muddy to the right of our neighborhood had a romantic look that day. Its great clumps of vegetation, flotsam, and banana cargo boats drifted along with the current towards the main city piers a quarter mile to the south.

A bus raced around the plaza trying to beat the time clock in the *tienda*, the store, at the other side. After it passed, I stepped into the street and a group of children in school uniform ran up to me, and tapped my arms as they went by.

"*Buenas tardes, Niña Caitlina,*" they sang in unison. Good afternoon.

The community center sat at the bottom of the hill. A high cement-block wall surrounded the yard and building. Rina Gomez stood waiting for me at the green, corrugated metal gate. As I climbed the short flight of stairs from the curb, I thought how pretty she looked in her starched, yellow cotton dress. She lived high up on the hill, close to the top, where the poorest shacks were. They had no running water, no electricity. But her clothes were never wrinkled, never dirty. Her straight black hair was always shiny and perfectly in place. Only her skin and her teeth gave away how poor she was. Her face was a sallow brown, and scarred a darker shade from pimples and smallpox. Her teeth were all gone and she wore an ill-fitting form of false teeth that she'd saved years to buy.

"Caitlina," she hugged me, throwing her large arms around my shoulders and pressing her full breast against me. She would greet me twice a day like this and then would grab my arm and hang on. In the beginning, so much affection had bothered me, but I'd grown used to it, and that afternoon it was a comfort.

We walked arm in arm through the gate into the inner courtyard, and across its dusty expanse to the rough wood structure that was the center. Inside, the women had shoved the desks from the preschool class over to the back wall and sat at their sewing machines in the center of the large room. They waited for Rina to distribute the pieces for the mosquito nets. The women earned three sucres for each net they made, and the community center two. This equaled fifteen cents to the center's ten. If they worked hard they could make a dollar a week, and the community center about eighty cents per woman.

"Como esta tu commandante?" How is your commander? Sra. Rodriguez called over to me from where she was settled in. She was a heavy woman who I always thought was pregnant, but who never seemed to give birth. She was referring to the commander of the Ecuadorian navy. She asked this every day. It was the affectionate joke of the neighborhood. The naval base was across the plaza from the center. The commander had taken a liking to me that I hadn't discouraged, although I'd never given him any opportunity to make his move. He let the community kids play basketball on their grounds. I repaid the favor by teaching an English class to his officers and trading flirtatious repartees with him in front of the recruits.

"As cute as ever," I said.

Sra. Rodriguez laughed, opening her mouth wide. The other women laughed, too, and shook their right hands in the air so the index finger hit against the middle one, making a loud smack.

Soon everyone was bent over their fluff of white. Black hair enfolded in gossamer. Behind them the cement wall, washed in turquoise, rose fifteen feet over their heads. A slight breeze blew through the room. The machines whirred, the pedals pumping at an extraordinary speed. I just sat, taking this all in, letting it melt away my anger at Bob Stevens.

After Rina finished tabulating who had what, she said she needed to go over the center's books with me. Reluctantly, I got up from my seat. I had become sleepy, hypnotized by the sound and movement. I followed her into the dark, adjoining room. Rina opened the wooden door and unlatched the shutters on the windows, letting in heat and light. As I waited for her to find her place in the ledger books, I thought with pride that when I'd arrived this had been nothing but a shell of a building. In the short time I'd worked with people here, we'd finished the construction, set up a self-governing board of directors, and gotten the *centro communal* to a place where we no longer had to take money from the North American-backed Kiwanis Club that had funded the project. All in a year and a half. Bob Stevens couldn't possible have done better than that.

"The membership is up by ten people this month, Caitlina," Rina said.

I yawned. *"Que bueno,"* I said, trying to get my mouth closed. That's great.

"Caitlina, bomba," she said. Caitlin, idiot. "I need you awake and serious to do this with me."

"You don't need me. You do this better than I do. Every time we compare addition, I'm wrong."

"You only try to be wrong to prove to me that I'm not stupid," Rina glared.

"Como tu quieres." What do you want? I said and laughed. Rina couldn't be fooled by my organizer's manipulation. She was too skilled an organizer herself. She was one of the two people I knew could take over for me when I left. The other was Hermes Castro, the president of the center.

I had no choice but to check her addition. She also made me count all the money in front of other people before she put it in the bank. According to Rina, only a gringo witness could prevent the others in the neighborhood from accusing her of taking money for herself. Her last vestige, I thought, of old ways of thinking.

"Sra. Alvarez, cinco sucres. Sra. Milagro, cinco sucres. Sr. Davila, cinco sucres." Rina read aloud through the hundred or more names as I wrote down the amounts. Then in silence, I added. Rina got up and went into the room where the women were sewing. The room I was in grew hotter as the afternoon sun moved deeply into it.

"Cinco, diez, quinze," I counted in my head. *"Veinte, veinte-cinco, trente."*

One morning a week later, I was making milk for the children's snack with a group of mothers. We worked like this every day in the cooking classroom, while the *jardin des infantes,* the kindergarten, went on in the class next door. As Sra. Mirales and I carried the heavy pot of water from the kerosene stove to the counter, I could hear the children singing, *"La Naranja, tan bonita . . . ,"* the orange, so beautiful, at top volume. We carefully poured the steaming water into a huge bowl of powdered CARE milk while Sra. Davila stirred it with a wooden spoon. I started back with the empty bowl when two boys from the center's soccer team appeared at the open window.

"They're here, the gringos are here," they said breathlessly. "With a million presents for us."

I looked out the window and saw men in naval dress uniform carrying cartons in through the green gate. Word had spread to high on the hill and more than twenty people from the neighborhood had already gathered in the yard. Quickly, I went into the classroom and told the teacher to keep the children inside.

As I walked across the dirt yard, people were jamming through the gate. Young men and boys scrambled over the wall. Unable to get by, all I could do was look over people's heads out to the street. There I saw an open flatbed truck, twenty feet long, piled high with riches: blond wavy-haired dolls, wearing organdy party dresses, taller than any ten-year old Ecuadorian child, cartons of toothpaste, boxes of basketballs, rolls of fabric.

People pushed by me. I heard them say, "You lied to us. *La mentira*. Liar. You said you'd bring nothing. But now you are good. We knew you'd be a good girl." I tried to answer, but nobody wanted to listen.

A navy man carried in a bolt of brocade, its deep blue background woven through with a lush red. Sra. Paredes, a little, fat, batlike woman I'd never liked, who never came to the center and only talked against it, grabbed at the material and brought it down into the rising dust. She was picking it up when someone else went for it, yelling at her, "Leave the things alone, this is for everyone. The Niña Caitlina has to tell us what to do." But that didn't stop Sra. Paredes, who was down again like a linesman over her property.

The young innocent-faced navy men continued to carry the goods in. They were followed now by the grinning Bob Stevens, proudly rising to his toes so that he appeared taller than those surrounding him. And in his mouth, the cigar.

Our courtyard was full, but people continued to push in. I saw Hermes Castro, our president, coming toward me. Rina Gomez was with him. I almost started to cry. Off to the side, people were scuffling over the dolls.

"What's going on?" Hermes yelled, his usually gentle face rigid with anger.

"I told them not to come." He couldn't hear me.

"Tell them to get out of here," he shouted.

I turned to Bob Stevens who stood a few feet away. "Get this shit out of here!"

His face went pale with shock. I don't know if it was from my tone, or from what he was seeing. Women were now punching other women. Men were pushing men and women to the ground. I saw blood spurt from a boy's nose. An old woman wailed. She was on the ground covered with the gray loose dirt, a deep gash in her forehead.

"Look what you did," I screamed. "Look what you did."

The young navy men stood paralyzed. Their fair faces flushed red, like boys after a hard game. Rina Gomez came and stood between us.

"We have to get these things inside," she said. "Caitlina, do something. Make them take it all inside the center."

Standing there, I let out a wordless scream at the top of my lungs the way a child will do who has no words against the abuse of the world. And then I found the words. "Get this shit into our stockroom. I don't care how you do it. Just get it in there."

Hermes directed the operation. I see him now standing on the steps leading to the storeroom in his white *guayabera*, short jacket, streaked with blood and dirt, and his black pants gray with dust. His usually carefully combed hair fell into his face as he beckoned the navy boys to carry everything inside. They spoke no Spanish. Some other men from the neighborhood came to his aid, mostly I suspected to steal a little bit for themselves. I didn't really care. I watched people escape over the wall with bolts of cloth and giant dolls. Pieces of other dolls lay in the dirt. A blonde head here. A leg there. Scraps of a dress.

Rina stayed beside me and pushed people away. I was struck a few times, but so were others. When the yard had somewhat cleared, I sent word to get the children out. They left unharmed, guarded by the teacher and Sra. Mirales and Sra. Davila.

Hermes clamped the padlock on the storeroom door as people stood sullenly around the yard. Rina told me to tell the *Americanos* to leave. But I didn't have to. A moment later Bob Stevens came to tell me they'd have to be going. I said, "Good." But I didn't look at him. I turned and walked away.

Then the neighborhood people started to move toward me like an accusing chorus.

"When are you going to give us our things, Caitlina?"

"They're ours. They brought them for us."

"What a bad girl you are not to give them."

I began to answer, but I saw hatred in their brown faces as they advanced. The next thing I knew, Hermes and Rina were hurrying me up the stairs of the center and inside. They padlocked the windows and door, shutting everyone out but the three of us and four or five of the people who helped out in the melee.

"She can't go out there," I heard them say, even though they spoke in whispers. "She'll be harmed if she goes out there."

So we sat in the darkness. The only light came from the cracks in the rough wood of the walls and from the holes in the corrugated ceiling high above us. Tiny spotlights touched the tops of the desks we sat in. I could smell the milk that had never been drunk. Overhead stones were hailing down, setting up a din as they hit the metal roof.

Rina moved her large body into the school desk where I sat and held my hand. She didn't say anything. The room grew hotter with no air coming in. Gradually the stones on the roof stopped, and the angry voices subsided, until there was only the silence of the noon hour. Still we didn't speak. Rina rubbed the top of my hand. Hermes got up and walked to the door and opened it. He stood in the bright light, looking out for a long time. Then he came and sat down in the desk beside mine and leaned his elbows on his knees. His eyes were sad.

"I think it is safe for you now. *Pero tenga cuidado*. But be careful. I don't think you should go to your house now. Maybe you should leave the neighborhood for a while."

They took me to the bus stop and waited with me. It was lunch and siesta time. Everyone had gone back to their homes. As I rode out on the bus to the suburb where the Peace Corps office was, I closed my eyes and let the wind blow my hair. I pretended that nothing had happened, that the next few hours would go on forever. I don't know why I chose to go to the Peace Corps office. I suppose it was because it was the one place where Ecuadorians wouldn't be.

When I arrived, only the Peace Corps doctor and secretary were there. I went directly into the back room and curled up on the couch. The doctor came in for a moment.

"You okay, Cait?" he asked.

I kept my eyes closed and just nodded.

"I hear it was pretty rough out there today."

"It didn't have to be," I said. "Where's Stevens now? Out in another barrio destroying things?"

"He's in barrio El Cisne, I think."

"Jeezus."

He didn't say anything and I kept my eyes closed. I heard his feet shuffle on the terrazo floor.

"Maybe it's best you get some rest," he said. "I'll be in my office."

I didn't answer. He left. I laid there in the relative coolness of that back room and drifted off into a daydream of coming back to my neighborhood to find that the community had rallied behind me. People came to apologize for their behavior and to bring back what they had taken. Even those like Sra. Paredes who'd never joined the center decided to do so now in recompense for the damage they had done. I fell asleep.

When I woke, my blouse and skirt were soaked with sweat. I didn't know where I was. When I recognized the back room of the office, I even wondered what I was doing there. Then remembering, I sat up. I saw the mob of people coming after me. I couldn't go back. But where would I go if I didn't return? Oh, how I wanted to leave for home. I'd go to the airport and get on any plane, promising to pay when I got to New York. Or I'd put a call through on shortwave radio to my parents, saying to wire money. I could wait overnight in the office, or better, in the airport.

The tears began to pour out. I tried to keep the noise of my sobs back. I picked up the damp pillow and put it over my face. I cried softly after a while and thought of going to Quito or the shore for a few days. But I knew I wouldn't. I couldn't leave Rina and Hermes, and I would only be more frightened going back to the hill after a longer absence.

I dried my eyes on the hem of my skirt. I got up and went over to the window and looked out onto the dark tangle of the courtyard garden. I thought how wonderful it would be to live in comfort here in a house like this one. Under those circumstances, I could love this country.

I walked out through the office. The secretary was at her desk clattering away on her typewriter. The room was dim. She never had any light on at this time of day in order to keep cool. I didn't say goodbye or look into Bob Stevens' office. I just went out the front door into the intense heat of the afternoon.

By the time the bus pulled into Santa Ana Plaza, everyone's siesta was over. There was a mob around the wall of the center. Rina and Hermes stood against the green gate, a little higher than the others, arguing with people. My whole body was shaking as

I got down from the bus and walked toward them. Across the plaza. Across the street. Rina spotted me first. Then Hermes saw me. He looked frightened. People turned towards me. I kept walking. People came at me screaming. "Liar," they yelled. "Robber. Filthy prostitute gringa."

I started up the curb stairs. A child I didn't know grabbed my arm. She was about seven and wore a many times patched blouse and skirt.

"Good Niña," she whined. "Give me a gift."

Sra. Marta, the old lady who lived across the hall from me, attached herself to my other arm. She patted my breast.

"I'm your friend, Niña Caitlina, my beautiful gringita. You'll give me a present, I know."

People all around picked up the begging.

"Please, a little gift," they said, their heads inclining to the right, their hands outstretched.

I wanted to scream at them and hit them and make them take their clutching hands off me.

Rina was by my side. She pried the fingers off of my arms. Off of my shoulders. Hermes was in front of me, shoving people away. I noticed that he'd changed his shirt into a clean blue *guayabera*.

"Why did you come, Caitlina?" Rina was crying as she held onto my upper arm. I could feel her solidness against me. She put her face into my shoulder, moistening my blouse with her tears.

"I'm afraid," she whispered.

The crowd pressed in until their faces were so close I could feel their breath and smell the sweat of their bodies. The odor of poverty was overwhelming, of old cooking grease, and bad water, and not being able to bathe properly. A stone hit the back of my head and I stumbled. Turning, I yelled for them to stop. I yelled for silence.

"*Silencio*," Hermes shouted with his arms outstretched, in front of my face. Silence. "*Silencio*, the Niña Caitlina wants to speak."

"*Silencio, silencio*," passed through the huge mob.

"Move back. Move back." Hermes pushed at the chests of the men who were practically on top of us. I pushed, too. I felt the resistance of bones and flesh. But gradually there was breathing space. And silence.

"I came here to work in your neighborhood to help you to do the things you wanted to do." People began to grumble. A young man I knew to be one of the *marijauneros* spit on the ground in disgust. "I told you then that I didn't bring gifts or money, but only myself. It wasn't my idea that these things were brought into the neighborhood. It was my government." Noise rose from the crowd. I had to scream to be heard. "I'm not going to hand these things out . . ."

"Bitch."

"*Mentira.*" Liar.

"*Ladrón.*" Thief.

Fists were being shaken in my face. I could still feel Rina holding tightly to my arm. Hermes turned to me.

"They aren't going to listen, Caitlin. This is making it worse."

But I didn't know what else to do. I had to convince them.

"You'll kill each other if I hand it out now. People won't get their fair share."

I could hardly hear my own voice.

"We're going to keep it in the center and hand it out little by little through the center. Everyone will get something."

The last no one heard through the roar. Someone shouted that they should take it themselves, and the mob turned from me and raced back to the entrance of the center. They picked up rocks and began throwing them at the solid gate. Some of the men began to tear at the metal. Uselessly, they ran into it with their shoulders. A group of boys and men made a human stepladder and were sending people over the wall.

"We have to stop them," Hermes said. "We can't let them destroy the center."

I looked at his dark eyes, so pained and serious. If it meant so much to him, I had to think of something.

"I'm going for Commandante Guzman."

I ran acros the plaza as fast as I could, feeling the wind stirred hot on my skin, hearing the jeers of the mob behind me and the banging of rocks on the metal door. So it's come to this, I thought.

When I got to the entrance of the naval yard, the commandante was already driving toward me in his jeep.

"My little gringita with the big tears. I've never seen you so gentle till now. Get in." He grinned, showing his handsome white teeth under a thick mustache.

I began to explain. But he'd been watching it all, he said, and was coming to put a stop to it. He gestured back with his thumb. Sure enough, there was a group of twenty naval recruits, marching in place, with guns with bayonettes fixed.

We drove slowly toward the hill as the recruits ran in formation behind us, shouting their *"uno, dos, tres."* Ahead I saw the mob split and move away from the door. Boys and men came tumbling over the wall out of the center. Part of me gloated in my power. Part of me prayed they'd all get out of there before there was trouble.

"Please," I said. "Don't harm anyone."

The commander grinned, but didn't look at me.

"Your commandante's not a fool, Caitlina. Unlike your navy boys. I don't desire to make things worse. I come only to bring the peace and to help out my favorite gringa. Maybe someday you'll repay me." He reached out and touched my knee.

By the time we pulled up to the wall of the center, the crowd was standing well away from the gate. The commandante got out of the jeep slowly, and came around to help me down. I had enough presence to wait for him. Rina and Hermes ran over.

"We've got to get everything out of there," Rina said. "It's not safe in the center and the center isn't safe with the things inside."

The commandante ordered his men to stand by the gate and spread out in a line across the bottom of the stairs, cordoning off the people. After giving the order he turned to me, raising his dark eyebrows in question.

"Can you put them in your storeroom?" I said, looking at the other two for agreement. They did agree.

"Your wish is my command, Señorita." He bowed.

Rina unlocked the green gate and pulled it open. The crowd moved closer to the guards. The guards raised their bayonetted guns to attention and the people froze. Even the children stood like statues, soundless.

I went with the commandante and Hermes and Rina into the courtyard. This was the hour for the machines to be whirring. Now there was only silence. Hermes went up the stairs to the storeroom. He stood with his back to us fumbling with the combination on the lock. He turned to look at me in desperation.

"I don't know, Hermes. I can't remember it," I said, listening for noise from outside the wall.

Finally, Hermes got the lock open and we went inside. The room was dark and hot. I pulled the light string. The commandante whistled.

"You're certain now, Señorita Caitlin, that you want us to move this?" For the first time in the year I'd known him, he spoke to me with the formal "you."

"Yes," I said. "We want it out of here."

And so the slow process of carrying the packages out our gate under armed guard, across the street, in through the gate of the Ecuadorian navy, began. I stood by the wall of the center through it all. Rina clutched my arm. Hermes stood a little apart, staring straight ahead.

"We'll bring them back soon," I said. "They'll see we aren't lying to them."

Rina screwed up her face, moving her mouth in an ugly manner, and spit. Her entire body shot forward with the force of the act.

"*Basura,*" she said. "Garbage. My people are garbage. I'll never work for them again."

"Rina, that isn't true. Their response is to be expected," I said, but when I looked at the faces of the people still hanging around, they looked ugly to me. I was furious at them once again. Why hadn't they learned the lessons I'd tried to teach them of dignity and self-reliance and belief in one another? When I realized the significance of my thought, I was shocked with myself. I was as arrogant as Bob Stevens.

"Hermes," I said, turning to him. "Tell her it's not their fault. If I had kept my director out of here, this wouldn't have happened."

He shook his head. "Everyone is wrong in this."

We walked up the hill together, Rina still clinging to my arms. We passed through the massed people. They muttered awful, filthy things to us, about each of us. They didn't dare strike out only because the commandante had left some recruits to guard the neighborhood for the night. We stopped at the door of my apartment. "Will you drink some coffee?" I asked. They both declined my offer.

That night I sat in my apartment with the lights turned out, watching as the people milled around the bottom of the hill, skirting the guards, forming little groups, talking.

After a few weeks, we began to filter the items through the programs. We picked up new members. Word went up the hill that they could get presents if they joined the *centro communal*. Even Sra. Paredes was a member for a month—until she didn't get the doll she wanted for her grandniece. People became nice, but they were obsequiously nice, humbling themselves before me, insinuating there were more gifts where these came from. But the worst was for Hermes and Rina. No one would believe they hadn't gotten more than everyone else. The two of them gradually became less active in the Center, giving up their leadership roles and only attending an occasional class or meeting.

I became too discouraged to continue and asked for a transfer. Hermes was right. We had all failed each other.

Letters Home

Wendy Polich

Dear Dad,

Happy birthday! If you were to have been born on this day in Paraguay, your name would have been Antonio because today is the birthday of Santo Antonio, and a holiday as well. There are a zillion saints here and everyone has their own saint. Every town has its own saint. November 19th is the birthday of Santa Isabel, so my name would have been Isabel—the same name as the leper colony 5 km from here. Of course Elena is a famous saint in Paraguay, so maybe she's my saint. Every house has a little shelf where they keep pictures of their saints and every night light a candle there. I know a kid named Domingo (born on Sunday) and another Viernes Santo (born on Friday during *semana santa*, saints week) and another named Bien Venido, which means welcome. This month there is a holiday called San Juan, and a huge fiesta of fire. They light soccer balls on fire and play, and they wave torches of straw and yell *"Viva Paraguay,"* climb greased poles to get to prizes, walk on hot coals, and ask San Juan what the weather will be like and who will marry who.

If you were to have been born in Paraguay, you would have been a soccer (*fútbol*) fanatic instead of a baseball or golf fanatic. You would go with your friends to the nearest house with a TV

Wendy Polich, a former Peace Corps volunteer, has traveled extensively in Africa, having grown up in Botswana, and lived in Cairo for a year. She is currently working on her medical degree at Tulane University, in conjunction with a masters degree in public health. She is married to a former Peace Corps volunteer and is the mother of a two-year-old son.

(there's one here in Cerro Verde), and watch the world soccer championships this month and cheer on Romerito, their famous player. You'd maybe watch the game three times in a row because they show it three times in a row. If you didn't go somewhere and watch the game or listen to it on the radio, you would know when a goal was made because you'd hear the cheers all over town. You'd be proud that so far Paraguay has won one game and tied two (once with Mexico, the former champs). You wouldn't have to work and the schools would all be closed.

If you were to have been born in Paraguay, you would go to school until the sixth grade where you would learn to speak Spanish but continue to speak Guaraní with your family and friends. You would learn all about your country's great war heros and how to follow and obey rules and those who are superior to you. If you could afford it, then you would go to the *colegio* (or high school). If you did go, you would probably leave the *campo,* the countryside, maybe go to Asunción or Buenos Aires, so you wouldn't have to work in the *chacras,* small fields. If not, you'd probably work in the *chacras* where you'd plant corn, beans, cotton, and manioc. You'd have an ox cart and maybe a horse, and go to fiestas, where you'd meet a girl and visit her on Tuesdays, Thursdays, and Sundays. You'd get married and have eight or ten kids. First, of course, when you were sixteen, you'd serve two years in the military and have a Mohawk hairstyle if you couldn't buy your way out. You'd have a big family with a lot of relatives and friends who were politically affiliated with you. You'd have to watch what you said and where you bought your meat and where you lived. If you lived in Cerro Verde, you'd probably be considered liberal or Communist, and if you went around holding meetings without permission or telling people to grow crops other than what the government wanted, you'd probably be put in jail. You'd always be watched. They might hold a mass for you if you were killed, though. You'd read papers and listen to news that was censored, but you probably wouldn't know it. You might have political power, or friends in high places. If not, you'd probably just work in your *chacras* and get paid very little by a government that put money in its own pocket.

You would have one good shirt to wear to special occasions and always wear a cowboy hat, you'd play poker with your friends, but with a deck of forty cards. You'd eat meat and manioc; meat killed the same day. You'd enjoy simple things: sleeping outdoors when it was hot or when there was a cool breeze, lots of relatives, smothering your little children with hugs and kisses and singing to them. You'd have a big party on your birthday, maybe kill some chickens, or better yet, a pig, but you'd sell half of it in town or to the neighbors. You'd know the seasons inside and out, you'd be affected by rain and drought. You'd drink *maté,* hot tea, in the mornings and *terere,* cold tea, with your friends after working in the fields. You'd know all your neighbors and greet them with "adios, amigo!" or give them your hand. You'd ask for a blessing every time you encountered an older relative. You probably wouldn't go to church, but you'd be a Roman Catholic.

You'd probably still work with wood if you were born in Paraguay. You'd chop it to clear fields, you'd sell it as firewood, fuel for the train, fuel for your meals, to build your house, bamboo for your fences. You'd make presses for alfalfa and *cana dulce* (sugar cane), and make beehives and hoes. You'd find pieces to carve figures of animals and paint them, or make wonderful inventive things out of nothing, because you'd have nothing. Your house would be bare of frills, you wouldn't be concerned about where you throw your garbage, but your dirt patio would always be swept clean every day. You'd know how to use a machete for anything.

You wouldn't have many teeth, or maybe you'd have false teeth. You wouldn't need glasses. You'd go to sleep when it's dark, get up when it's light. You wouldn't know what retirement meant. You'd work till you couldn't. You'd be hot in the summer and cold in the winter. You'd joke a lot and dance the polka under star-light and lantern light.

You might have a rich American live with you and pay room and board of $15.00 every month, and wonder what she's doing here so far from her family and all alone in a strange place. But you might start to get used to her and show her things that you thought were simple and ordinary but she thinks are very special. You might end up liking her and helping her out. You just might, wouldn't you? Sure you would. And on rainy days, sitting under the porch eaves, or on cold days, in the *cocina* (kitchen), sitting around the fire of the stove, you'd sip *maté* and sing or listen to the radio or tell stories and make her feel at home.

Happy birthday and happy Father's Day! Wish I could have spent them with you! All my love.

Wendy

CHAPTER 2

AFRICA

"Who Taught Those Chickens How to Swim?"

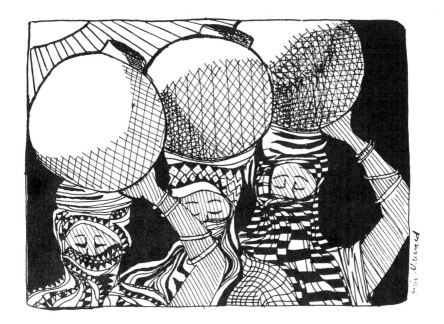

Marimanti. A village with such a jolly name deserves better than to exist in a gray fuzz of bush in the middle of the bush. Marimanti has one of the few bars I know where, to be assured of a cold beer, you have to supply five liters of diesel to start the generator. There is much livestock misunderstanding in these parts, as witness events when ducks were first released to augment the economy of the experimental fish ponds. The morning was rent by the anguish of an old man demanding to know "who taught those chickens how to swim?"

—John Makin

John Makin is an ecologist with the Natural Resources Institute in Chatham, Kent, United Kingdom. He has worked extensively in Asia, Africa, and the Middle East.

A Village Visit

Judith A. Graeff

People are very surprised to hear I'm going to spend time in a village. They question Kone, my guide, when the introductions and greetings are over. "What does she eat?" "She is so young!" "Why is she here? Does she think life in a village will please her?" "She *walked?*"

Later, after greeting people Kone knew in the village, I was given a bucket of hot water and shown where I could wash. They had built a small, roofless room of mud bricks with a tiny hole in the wall at the base. This was the drain. I washed and went to the bathroom, then washed it away with the remaining water in the bucket. It was quite a nice setup and I was relieved —I had heard stories of "everyone" going to the stream to wash. (I never actually lacked for privacy. I had the same bathing facilities in Diolisso, and had my own private hut for sleeping and dressing.)

Later, we ate dinner. They killed a chicken just for me, and Kone and I ate rice and sauce. The rest of the family ate *toh*, a wheat porridge, and sauce made of corn flour and water. I asked to join them, but Cisse, the host, was surprised to hear that I liked *toh*. I passed out cookies to everyone and we spent the evening chatting with the men. We also went into the kitchen where the women were and talked with them. That

Judith A. Graeff currently lives in Washington, D.C. and works in health communication for child survival, which keeps her in contact with Africa. Her international experience began twenty-five years ago as a Peace Corps volunteer in Côte d'Ivoire. Since then, she has obtained graduate degrees in behavioral psychology and public health.

night I slept alone in Cisse's room on a bamboo bed with a straw mattress. If a man has a bed, he also has bed curtains! I slept awfully well despite everyone's fear of mosquitoes.

Monday. We made it, but I sometimes wondered if we would. This morning, after two meals, Kone, Cisse, baggage, and I started out on two bicycles. I rode one bike with my suitcase strapped behind, everyone and everything else was on the other. They both doubted I could ride a bike, but later Kone said I was *trop forte,* very strong. Soon a mobylette overtook us, so at my insistence, Cisse went on ahead and Kone and I continued on the bikes. (Looking at the map later, we did about 10 km.) It wasn't a difficult ride, mostly downhill. However, we came to a big puddle—I chose the wrong side and landed, fortunately standing up, in the water. Kone pulled me out, but we couldn't stop laughing. Shortly, we reached Lokolo, and after 90 minutes, with the help of Cisse, we were able to negotiate a mobylette.

This started an incredible journey. It would have challenged the skill of a Hell's Angel, but I was driving! I had my suitcase strapped in front of me between the seat and handlebars, and Kone was sitting behind me holding his suitcase, my sack, and my camera. The trail was horrendous—there wasn't much to begin with, and much of what existed was either washed out or overgrown with grass. We had some pretty scary times, had to stop the bike and walk it, crashed into things, and were laughing like little kids. The path was no wider than one person on foot, and since it was a footpath, it curved and twisted all over the place. Then we came to the river, where there was a sharp drop of 50 or 60 feet. We managed to get the mobylette down, said hello to the women washing clothes, then Kone carried the mobylette across the river and I followed with the luggage. Once across, we had to get the bike up the same type of slope. Kone was pretty tired, but we did the same thing in reverse, helping another traveler.

The last 5 km were easier—the trail was wider, straighter, and smoother. Really a beautiful ride, and suddenly, there was Kone's village, tucked under the trees. We were met by six old toothless women. Their reaction to me is always lovely: their faces light up, their mouths drop open in a smile, and they clap their hands together in amazement. I can't understand a word they say, but their expressions are great! Kone's mother was in the fields so we went into his cousin's hut to wait for her. We sat awhile (with about a dozen kids looking on), then Kone left, and I slept on the bed in the hut. After a time, his mother came.

She is the person who fascinates me most of all the people I've met. I can't describe her well, but she is short with an average build (for someone who works fields by hand with a hoe, chops wood, carries water, and such), and she rarely smiles. Her manner was a bit bewildered: Here is a woman who hasn't left her village very often, has lost a husband, raised five children, works in the fields all year, and now her only son brings home a schoolteacher—someone from another world. I am a complete mystery to her. Hopefully we'll understand each other more by the end of the week. Right now things are a little awkward as she sits here in the hut with her small daughter and granddaughter, but Kone has gone to return the mobylette, and there is no way we can talk.

Tuesday. Last night Kone returned around 7:00 P.M. He and his friend repeated our trip in reverse to return the bikes and mobylette to their owners. The poor guy was exhausted. We stayed up until 10:00 P.M. with his sisters and others, sitting in my hut. He wanted to sleep this morning, but at 7:00 A.M., someone ran to wake him because they don't know what to do with me without him to translate. Two of his boy friends know French, so they help out in a pinch.

This morning Kone, his friend Mamadou, and I walked to some fields and watched people work. Generally they seem to work in the fields according to age and gender; that's how friends are arranged too. People don't work alone, but usually help each other on a rotating basis. Kone's two younger sisters go to the fields every day to work with other young girls; the time passes faster like that. His older married sister gave birth to her second child about ten months ago, so she is at home. Women return home for childbirth, and they stay until the baby can walk. This gives them a bit of vacation from their own homes and husbands, and it is a nice way for the woman's mother to enjoy her grandchildren.

We will probably go to the fields again this afternoon. Everyone here thinks I'm not used to getting any exercise at all, or working. I don't think I'll be allowed to lift a finger while I'm here. Also, my request to see the fields was not only met with surprise, but with the comment that they were too far away (a kilometer or two). Why does their work interest me? Most people tell Kone that he was crazy to bring me here—that they are poor and that I will suffer. They can't get over the fact that a white person actually wants to stay here awhile.

Last night and again this morning, we walked from hut to hut greeting people, with a twofold purpose. Kone needed to say hello to everyone since he was coming home for vacation, and he also had a guest to introduce. Greetings in Djoula are a dialog with certain phrases and responses to fit the occasion, the time of day, and the speakers. Many are benedictions: May God grant you. . . . In town there aren't more than two or three exchanges, but in the village, especially among the older folks, greetings can take a few minutes! People derive great pleasure from the routine and everyone was genuinely glad to see Kone again. They gave their greetings to me as well. The old women are so funny. You can hear them smack their toothless lips together and say, "For land's sake, Kone, what have you brought home with you? She's a pretty little thing!" Kone said most people thought I was beautiful: my teeth are straight, my hands are small (no farm labor). Many people also said I was very nice to come to their village to visit. Whites in the Côte d'Ivoire, unfortunately, have always demonstrated a very negative attitude about African ways of life, and these people were afraid I'd be scornful of their village. I am having a hard time convincing people (even Kone) that I'm not suffering and that I'm truly enjoying myself.

José

Linda Perkins

T he short, springy man appeared to lead the people, turning
and walking backwards to face them every now and then.
Chanting as he walked, calling people by name, he pushed his
military hat around as a shield from the sun. His treadless boots
poked out from dusty fatigues. Children followed him dressed
in genderless, hole ridden outfits. Babies, tightly wrapped in
African cloth, clung to their mothers. The group was a weary,
rumpled lot. They were heading for the American Embassy, and
only the leader seemed to know the way, and why.

Both Kitty and I had strong first impressions of Botswana.
The cat meowed mightily when my husband, Hank, picked us
up at Gaborone's airport. I wanted to get home quickly, but
Hank took a quick detour by the embassy, essentially to show
off his (and now my) new premises. Kitty squealed from her
carrier in the back seat.

"It's not a grand building," Hank said, as the familiar flag
came into view. "But I thought you'd like seeing it right away. We
installed a new flag yesterday; something festive for your arrival."

The dry, midmorning heat reduced the barren area surrounding the embassy to a single dimension. Stark, it resembled

Living abroad for twenty years, Linda Perkins has held a variety of positions
within American Embassies in addition to being a foreign service spouse. A
native of Seattle and a graduate of the University of Washington, she began
her international career in 1961 as an exchange teacher of English in Japanese
public schools. Subsequently, she worked in Brazil, Portugal, Mozambique,
South Africa, Botswana, Namibia, and Guinea-Bissau. She presently resides in
Washington, D.C.

nothing more than a partially finished wooden movie set for a desert film. A long, straggly line of African men, women, and children appeared to hold the building up—at least a hundred people or more. A new group joined the line as we drove past. The man leading them wore a distinctive military hat and alternately turned to face them and then to lead them.

"What's that crowd all about?" I asked. "Is that a bus stop?"

"Not exactly," Hank said, hesitantly. "Those are some of the refugees I told you about on the phone. You'll be working with them as refugee coordinator now that the embassy employment committee has picked you for the consular job."

"That's great. When do I start?"

"Right now, if you want. But don't you need to rest from your trip?"

"It looks like I'd better start right away if all those people are waiting for help!"

"Yes . . . but, prepare yourself . . . they're standing outside because the lobby is already overflowing with other refugees."

"You didn't mention numbers to me before," I gulped. "Who's been in charge till now?"

"John Bridges, the political officer, but he's swamped in his regular work. No one expected the number of refugees who'd apply for the resettlement program. Fortunately, the American Friends Service Committee opened a small living center recently, and they're doing some counseling, but none of them speaks Portuguese like you do. I've talked to two volunteers there, two Americans, and they're really looking forward to your arrival." All of this was certainly more than expected, I thought, as we drove through town.

At our new home several servants helped get our things from the car, and I removed Kitty's carrier from the back seat. They giggled as I carried it to a grassy area. Hopping out as soon as the lid opened, Kitty landed on the grass, shrieking as the long, clumpy *kikuyu* grass—so different from the grass she knew in Washington—rose up around her legs. With considerable aplomb for a weary traveler, she picked up her feet and fled to the house, quickly scrambling under a chair.

Within days, both Kitty and I had settled in. She overcame her hesitation to explore the garden when the first lilac-breasted roller flew by—a sensational pink and blue bird. Eventually, she lost her generic name and everyone called her "Mama Cat."

I, on the other hand, took up my station in the embassy file room, reading up on the refugee problem in the region. I hadn't realized, even while taking the Consular training in Washington, that I was on the brink of the second largest resettlement program in Africa. Recent humanitarian legislation in the United States, which had increased the number of refugees eligible to seek political asylum in America, was the main reason the embassy lobby was full.

The daily, desperate crowds of people had clearly created a stressful environment for everyone. The lobby was a small, sparsely furnished room with six or seven seats and a water fountain. It was separated from the consular office by a wall through which poked a glass-enclosed teller's window. The security door to the main part of the building was opposite this window, so all employees and visitors to the main embassy had to step around and nearly over the refugees on their way upstairs. Deborah, a timid consular assistant, had tried to discourage the refugees from waiting inside the embassy. She had told them she'd post a notice when I arrived, and appointments could be made then. But each day new groups waited, the men milling around inside, creating a continuum of raised expectations, while the women and children squatted on the curb outside.

On my first day in the extraordinarily cramped consular "cage," Deborah opened the curtain over the window as I arranged folders on top of my improvised desk. It was 10:00 A.M. and we were open for business. She handed me the list of names, arranged in alphabetical order, saying: "I hope it's a workable system, at least to get you started. We've never done this before, so I wasn't sure how to proceed. I posted a notice outside, so almost everyone knows when they're supposed to come in."

By 3:00 P.M., when we closed the consular curtain, I had spoken with thirteen refugees, some with families, some without. I found the awkwardness of their village Portuguese mixed with my rusty language skills dragged most appointments on longer than planned. Midway through the day, Deborah motioned to me as a new face peered into the consular window.

"That's one of the leaders," she said. "He's eager to speak with you alone. He's been in many times." Nodding in his direction, Deborah opened the door, and closing it softly behind her, I was left alone with him.

He was the man in the military hat, which he now held in his hand. He looked like a leader. Dressed in reasonably fresh fatigues and highly polished shoes, he nearly snapped to attention as he reached to shake my hand.

"Bom Dia, Senhora. E un grande prazar encontrar com a Senhora finalmente. Eu sou Commandante José Arriaga, as suas ordems!" Good day, Senhora. It is a great pleasure to finally meet you. I am Commander José Arriaga, at your service!

Surprised by his courtly ways, I urged him to take a seat. We exchanged a few more pleasantries, then he began to tell his story. Apparently, his rank hadn't shielded him from the atrocities I was hearing daily. In fact, most of what he recounted justified any country's humanitarian effort to provide a "safe haven" outside the war fields of Angola. He spoke earnestly in fluent Portuguese.

"I've been here nearly two months," he said, leaning forward in his chair. Almost whispering, he was clearly used to being careful. "Several hundred came with me, but some have gone back. Life is not easy here, either." He shrugged. "More than ten families I know have gone back; some have returned. At one time, we hoped the international powers would get a truce going, but it looks hopeless now. The Cuban troops, supported by the other side, haven't left our region. There's constant looting, raping, death squads; no one knows what each day will bring. My region is one of the poorest, so bringing this hardship on us, along with no food except what we can grow. . . . Well," he sighed, "you've heard our plight. Anything should be better. But you know, Botswana isn't a developed country either, and when it comes to poor people, if you're not from here, you have difficulty. When we heard that America might have room for us—such a big country—we got excited."

I was getting excited, too; Commandante José articulated the situation well, and mindful of new information, I took detailed notes. The human face he put on this tragedy helped in many ways. Speaking with conviction, the commandante took on an incredible resemblance to one of the more charismatic leaders of the struggle, Jonas Savimbi.

"How are you managing here?" I asked, putting my notes aside for a moment.

"I was a mechanic before the war, and my parents ran the local cantina. I fixed up old trucks and went all over the country picking up scrap metal, food, and giving people rides. I speak seven African languages. I'm sort of doing the same thing here. An Angolan friend married a local woman and he's been here for years. He lets me use his backyard for my work. My family's all there, in the backyard. We go to the center now and then, but mostly I help the others. You know, there're many different languages, and I speak them all. I never have any—what shall I say —I don't have any time on my hands!" With that, he raised his large hands up. I could see from the rounded palms and thick fingers they were immensely capable. His lean body and bright eyes framed an internal energy. Outwardly simple in appearance, he registered a ten on my survivor scale. Though he'd traveled great distances he hadn't lost his sense of direction.

During the first years of the war, he continued, he had been sent to Portugal and traveled through other parts of Europe as an emissary, but Africa always called him back. Now displaced, he was trying to make a go of it in Botswana. With two wives, nine children, several brothers and their families, a cousin, and his aged father, he'd traveled many miles to a freer climate. Finally, as our interview grew to a close, he spoke of his relationship with the beleaguered leader of the *Frente Nacional de Liberacao de Angola* (FNLA), his commander in chief. Serious disappointment colored his voice, as he spoke of his decision to flee.

Regrettably, I realized it was way past time for the next interview. As I shook his strong hand, I agreed to meet him and his family the following Friday afternoon. Closing the door behind him, I wondered how the Immigration and Naturalization Service (INS) officer would deal with this incredible man and his two wives.

Obviously, determining the refugees' eligibility, preparing case histories, and performing preliminary medical tests for the INS visit in two months was going to take time. The initial interviews and paperwork demanded thoroughness. Providing the INS officer with information he or she needed to make final decisions about who would go to the United States was a heavy responsibility. I had to distinguish between those who actually faced persecution or death if returned to Angola and those who were fleeing economic and social turmoil. The first forty or so interviews indicated that the least of the problems ahead would be the physical and mental health of each person, most of whom were severely undernourished. Some were emotionally unstable, suffering from shell shock and other traumas. In addition, I knew job opportunities in the States would be problematical; the war in Angola had left most refugees bereft of schooling or training. They were trained only for war. Finally, helping the American sponsoring agencies locate families willing to care for and monitor the adjustment of the refugees seemed a formidable task.

Angolan refugees formed the majority of my cases. Fleeing their civil war, the men were mostly simple foot soldiers, snagged into this long fight more by proximity than principle. Leaving their country with women, children, and a few possessions meant walking more than a thousand miles from their villages, a journey made more difficult by walking at night. While still in occupied territory, the dark allowed freedom of movement; but once in Botswana, the night was only a shelter from the heat of the Kalahari Desert. Disasters haunted them: sickness, lack of food, and the nocturnal leopard, as well as other predators, that occasionally snatched a small child or someone weakened by sickness. Scattered and disparate, the groups were led by men like José, who'd served together in the troops or came from the same village. Often, they'd lose contact. One group had last been seen clinging to the tops of sparse trees waiting for a pride of lions to pass.

By the end of the week, I was considerably cheered by a visit to Al and Sandy Lawson at the Friend's Center. I had no trouble finding the place. It wasn't the crowd standing around—many of whom I recognized in the fading evening light—that marked the spot, but the well-lighted hall built in fresh pine with an enormous thatched roof.

"Park over there," Al said, when he met me at the gate. "Sandy and I want to give you a quick tour before dark."

Everything was rustic, from the single-sex, tin-roofed dormitories on dirt courtyards swept clean by twig brooms, to the small outdoor ablution areas with no running water. Al gestured toward the various small buildings, explaining that the center was all part of a self-help project they had designed. It was built entirely by refugees, he said proudly. The meeting hall, which we now approached, served as the center of activity, from simple food preparation and dining to just sitting around. Pointing to a large field still being cultivated by refugees as the last light left the sky, Al said, "That's where we spend most of our time. The drought created many problems. Often there's no water, and we can't count on electricity most of the time.

Fortunately, one of the refugees—I don't know if you've met him yet, but he's our genius—always gets the pump working again. The pump's a German donation but, of course, it didn't come with extra parts. This man, José, is a virtual spark plug for us here—he never gives up!"

"Is that genius José Ariaga?" I asked, already sure of the answer.

"Yes. Have you met him?"

"I certainly have. He was in the office today. What a guy! I saw over sixty refugees today and Commandante José stood out. It's not his rank or language ability, there's something else so strong there—no wonder all the others lean on him. I'm hoping he'll help when the INS man arrives. José's so articulate he gives life to the stories others just tell."

"He's quite a man. Listen," Al said, turning from the field, "Sandy and I talked after meeting you today, and we're both impressed with your practical outlook. We could work well together. Why don't you interview people at our center? You're incredibly cramped at the embassy and we've got plenty of room. Most of the Angolans come by on a regular basis, anyway. Sandy and I work mostly with those starting a new life here in Botswana, you know. Although we recognize the U.S. goal is to resettle as many as possible in the States, we feel moving many of them out of Africa into a new world, knowing that it might be hostile, isn't always the best. Anyhow, you're more than welcome to join us here."

Taken with their sincerity and the ample space, I soon moved all processing activities to the center. Commandante José worked his magic there, as well. Communicating with everyone, in many different tongues, he brought a special order to our efforts. Daily, he careened into the parking lot in a newly fixed truck jammed with refugees. He worked long, hot hours repairing yet another mechanical glitch, translating for me, or just taking a moment to console someone. His energetic love of life imparted an infectious hopefulness to the project. If asked about his own well-being, or that of his family, he brushed aside any questions with an exuberant flippancy.

"I don't have any time on my hands!" he'd say. With this colloquial turn of phrase, he always extended his hands in the air, waving his palms toward the sky.

The pending visit of the INS officer, Mr. Innes, grew nearer. As the final countdown approached, one of the leaders committed suicide, a sad and almost unheard of resolution of inner agonies in Africa; several women gave birth and many more announced their pregnant status; two young men were picked up by the police for drunkenness and jailed; one child died of a fever; three men didn't pass their physicals when syphilis showed up on their blood smears, and a few decided to go "missing." From the original 259 cases, I ended up with 210 ready to see Mr. Innes, a person now grown extremely large in stature to them.

I remember well my conversation with José at the center as he helped me move my files into the car the night before Mr. Innes' arrival. Moving gingerly, he was careful not to appear too curious about the contents of my confidential files. He wanted to say something, though. It was written on his face.

"Mama Linda," he said, using the name the refugees had given me. "What will happen tomorrow? Do you still want me to help translate?" Hearing in his voice more than just concern for his compatriots, I knew he wondered what would happen to him and his family the next day. During our original interview he had been extremely straightforward about his two wives, neither of whom was secondary to the other. I could still hear his description. "You may have difficulty understanding two wives," he had said that day. "But it's very easy for me to understand, and they do, too. What can I do? I've heard one cannot go to America with two wives, but I wouldn't go if I couldn't take both. This is my family, after all." I had no answer for him then or now. Without José helping people through their medical appointments, translating for them, driving them to the center to work, caring about their everyday concerns, we just wouldn't be so ready.

"Yes, José," I said, as we approached the car. "I want your help tomorrow and the next day, as we discussed. Be sure your family is ready for their interview. And try not to worry. Just present your case and hope for the best." I knew I couldn't interfere with Mr. Innes' final decision.

As we finished packing my car, Al appeared from the garden to open the gate. Brushing dried soil from his hands, he reached out to pat my back.

"I hope things go well tomorrow. You've done a lot to make life more bearable for many here. You've treated everyone with dignity and respect, and that's done a lot for their recovery, too." It seemed ironic he was directing his comments to me when, just at that moment, the lights in the meeting hall flickered to life, starkly illuminating both his and José's faces.

"Red" Innes, a west Texan, brought years of experience along with gritty pragmatism to his work the next day. "You know, Linda," he drawled, "I'll be back before you know it. But we'll do what's possible in my two days. Your files look thorough, and I know you want to see these cases resolved, but it all takes time. So let's begin, and we'll just let those ole chips fall where they may!"

José, dressed in freshly washed fatigues, ushered in the first case and took a seat at the far side of the conference table. Becoming almost invisible, he proved indispensible when translations became necessary. Surprisingly, I never got the feeling during those first hours that something was happening to him. Not when each applicant was sworn in, not even when their specific stories touched on his experiences did I sense that José was losing energy. Apparently, though, their stories drained him, like a battery going dead.

We broke for lunch, but it wasn't until the late afternoon that José beckoned to me; he was obviously agitated. Though Red chose not to inform anyone of their status after the interview, leaving that for a later date, many refugees remained in the building milling around.

"Can I speak with you alone?" José asked. He was standing next to the door as I came in.

"Yes, of course. What's the matter? You look different. Are you feeling all right?"

"I'm all right, but I've made a big decision and it hurts to do it."

"What do you mean?

"I think my decision is that I'm not going to take someone else's place. I'm not going to America."

"José, how can you say that? You don't know if you'd be approved or denied. Why not talk to Mr. Innes and see what happens? Isn't your family waiting outside?"

"Yes," he said, looking at the door. "I know this man seems a good person, but I've made up my mind. Listening to the others, I just feel they deserve more of a chance. They've never had anything but war, and I've had good luck some of the time. You know me, I'm an African through and through, and I'd better stay here. I'll go on helping you and my family can stay in João's backyard."

Red motioned he was ready to resume. José followed me into the room and, noticeably more relaxed, took his seat. Surprised by his change of mind, part of me was glad he'd be around to help. But remembering the crowded backyard, I wondered if he wasn't making a rash decision. Making his case now, with Red, might serve him better—two wives or not—then being questioned later. Several cases took his place, though, and it was only after we left the building around 7:00 P.M. that I could speak to him.

"José, are you sure about this? Did you talk to your family?"

"Yes, I'm sure, and no, I didn't talk to them. I know I can do more here than anywhere," he said, gesturing. "Besides, I don't want any time on my hands."

The first refugees bound for the States left three months later. Of the 210 cases presented to Red that first session, 161 were successful. Of those, most were truly deserving of a fresh start; maybe a few who were less qualified slipped through, but we worked hard to verify all cases. I'll never forget that group's departure. Zambian Airlines arranged for a larger plane than usual to ferry them out of the country. All 161, with families pushing the figure to over 280, departed for Lusaka. Continuing the journey the next day by jumbo jet, they would arrive in New York in the dead of winter, forty-two hours after seeing the sun set in Gaborone.

I arrived at the airport early, with a long clipboard in hand. The small departure lounge was already bursting with people, forcing many well-wishers to stand outside. Parking my car, I heard calls to "Mama Linda." Since this was a chartered flight, we had the airport to ourselves. Al and Sandy scurried around, helping some of their hardest workers close bulging suitcases. None had been on a plane before, and as the engines warmed up on the tarmac, several young people joked nervously, gesturing towards the exit. We knew José would be transporting twenty people from town, destined for this flight, but none of us were prepared for the sight of his small truck filled to overflowing with the twenty and at least twenty more. Honking as he approached the entrance to the airport, he narrowly missed a stray goat on the road.

Once everyone was assembled and counted, the flight attendants moved them through to the departure enclosure. A regularly scheduled flight was due any moment and they rushed to free the airport of this crowd. Al and Sandy helped me check that papers were in order. José cajoled those timid in boarding such a large ferry, laughing as he moved them along. Suddenly, the building was empty. Al, Sandy, and José went outside to watch the plane take off. I'll never forget seeing José, as I drove away, standing on the flatbed of his truck, waving with his palms facing up, long after the plane had left the local skies.

Two years later, Hank and I readied ourselves for departure. We'd miss many parts of our life in Botswana, but most of all we were going to miss our friends. For me, the urgency and gratification of working with refugees wouldn't be duplicated anywhere else. The center had become a second home. José, Al, Sandy, and I were often there together, helping refugees and occasionally sharing letters received from the new American residents. Though none of us was ever sure that all of those who went—six hundred, give or take a few—found happiness, we knew we'd tried to help.

As we pulled away from the house, Mama Cat crouched low in her carrier in the back seat of the car. I knew that looking back at the people standing there would make me cry again. Kitty howled for us all. Hating airport goodbyes, I was hoping no one would show up for ours. I wanted to slip away. I'd already said goodbye so many times at this airport, I didn't want it to happen again. But that was not to be. Even the airport personnel showed up to wish us "God's speed!" I tried to busy myself with the cat carrier, but even that job was taken from me by well-wishers. I don't remember much about all the hand-shaking, kissing, and crying, except that it was emotional. But I do remember looking back on the airfield, our plane banking to the west, and seeing Al, Sandy, and José, standing tall on the back of José's flatbed truck in what had by then become a famil-iar pose. Even now, I can see them in my mind's eye, waving vigorously, each with their palms turned to the sky, José's arms seeming to me then to reach even higher than all the others.

Soul to Soul

Alison Tinsley

"Your adoring fans are sure gonna appreciate the care you're taking with your makeup." Z Raymo was tall, black, muscular, and unamused.

"*Quoi?*" What? Holding her mascara wand at a dainty angle, Natalie looked up at Z from under thick, black lashes. Her innocent eyes were startlingly lavender. She understood Z perfectly; her father worked at the American Embassy and her English was as good as mine.

"Come on, guys. There isn't any point in sitting here bickering. We might as well walk a ways." I heaved myself off my backpack and hoisted it up. Z glared at me, then resumed reading his book. Natalie flicked a perfectly manicured hand in a gesture of dismissal. I sat back down.

Oh my God, I groaned internally. What had I done to deserve getting stuck hitchhiking to a rock festival in Ghana with a radical black Peace Corps volunteer and a vacationing French model? Well, to begin with, I'd invited them both to go with me.

I'd been living in the Ivory Coast for a week when I'd heard about the three-day festival sponsored by MGM. Santana would be there, and Roberta Flack, along with many other

---

Alison Tinsley, the daughter of a foreign service secretary, lived and traveled extensively in Europe while growing up. After graduating from college, she worked for the Peace Corps and taught English in West Africa, where travel continued to be one of her favorite activities. She recently moved to Frederick, Maryland, from her home in New Mexico. She has taught high school and college writing, written newspaper and magazine articles, received awards for her short stories, and is currently working on two mystery novels.

popular American and African musicians. What an opportunity. My job with the Peace Corps didn't start until the following Monday and the map indicated that Accra was only about one hundred, max two hundred, miles away. Piece of cake, I thought. I'll hitchhike. But maybe I should take someone with me. I'll ask around. That, I ruefully remembered, was how I'd ended up here, with these two people I barely knew.

My companions—neither of whom had been in Africa much longer than I—had never met before we'd joined up at 8:00 A.M. that Friday at the taxi stand just south of Abidjan. Their reaction to each other had been instant, intense dislike. All day, Z had snapped at Natalie, she'd pretended not to understand him while simultaneously provoking him unmercifully, and I'd tried to mediate between the two of them. What hadn't helped the situation any was that, for the past four hours, we'd been sitting at the border between the Ivory Coast and Ghana. It was so hot and buggy that our sweat formed little swimming pools in which mosquitoes frolicked, gleefully swan diving and back flipping onto our dripping bodies.

After our initial good luck in getting a ride with two Canadians to a volunteer organization encampment about 3 km from the border, we'd struck out. We'd walked the final distance. At the border, two guards had, after carefully examining our documents and directing us to fill out several forms in triplicate, obligingly stamped our passports and told us we could cross into Ghana. Then we'd stepped over the imaginary line to wait for the next vehicle. Natalie filed her fingernails and Z paced. Half an hour later, I went back to the small border station to ask one of the guards how often cars came through here. *"Non, non,"* he scolded when I placed one foot on Ivorian soil. If I came back into the Ivory Coast, he explained, I'd have to go through all the paperwork again. And then do it again, if I wanted to return to Ghana. Hastily, I pulled my foot back.

"Combien de voitures?" How many cars? he repeated the question I had asked him, rolled his eyes and shrugged his shoulders. After serious consultation with his partner, they determined that maybe one car a day drove through this border. Another small glitch in my hitchhiking plan.

Determined not to lose my good humor, I returned to Z and Natalie. With three feet of unbridgable space between them, they both sat on their backpacks. Natalie was painting her nails with crimson polish, and Z was reading Che Guevara. I plopped down between them. Neither of them looked at me.

Now, three-and-a-half hours later, darkness—so rapid to advance this close to the equator—was settling in. Natalie did a final touch-up to her makeup while she could still see, Z got in a final sarcastic comment, and I volunteered my final, futile suggestion. Walking seemed better than sitting here—but where was there to walk to? We weren't even halfway to Accra, and it had taken us all day to get this far. We'd be lucky if we arrived at the festival before it was over Sunday evening.

The border guards waved, called, *"à demain,"* till tomorrow, and drove away. What did they mean, until tomorrow? Surely they weren't implying we'd be here all night.

Actually, they were.

It would be erroneous to say we woke up the next morning, because we never really slept that night. What we did was alternate between two states of misery. First, we sweated miserably in our sleeping bags while mosquitoes nibbled only on our necks and noses. Then, when the heat became unbearable, we threw our sleeping bags off to allow our exposed bodies to cool while mosquitoes devoured us completely. Mosquitoes buzzed as they dive-bombed our heads and whined as they flew in our ears. Other muted jungle sounds were punctuated by a long, loud, steady drone. One major, monster, mosquito. Needless to say, our tempers had not improved by morning.

Who knows what horrible acts we might have committed had not a vehicle appeared, obscured by a cloud of dust, coming down the dirt road toward us. "What is it?" Natalie asked eagerly, forgetting, for a moment, her sultry French accent.

"Maybe a bush taxi," Z answered, forgetting, for a moment, his sarcasm.

"It's a VW bus!" I shouted, when a familiar turquoise and white flat nosed form emerged from the swirling dirt.

"With German plates!" Natalie groped in her purse, withdrew a hairbrush, and began to style her tangled hair.

"They certainly won't give us a ride if your hair's not combed," Z said.

As the neon sun sank low in a haze-streaked sky, the van pulled up to a huge field in the center of Accra. My first impression was of hundreds of different rhythms pulsating down into the earth so that the ground seemed to vibrate. "Thanks again," we repeated over and over, as our two German saviors lifted our backpacks and sleeping bags out of the bus and handed them to us. "Thank you. Thank you."

Harmonies twined through the heavy air, surrounding us with sound. We stood on the edge of the crowd, a little dazed, smoke from hundreds of campfires blurring our vision in the dimming daylight.

"Later," Z said, and strode off toward the center of the action.

"Hey," I called to his retreating back. "Where are you going? Where should we meet?"

"Catch you back in Abidjan."

"*Cochon.*" Pig. Natalie stamped her foot like a five-year old about to throw a tantrum. "Get back here, *toute de suite!*" Immediately!

Z disappeared.

"Well, fine." Natalie threw her arms wide in a desperate gesture. "Here we are, two helpless women. How could you have let him leave?" From her pocket, she extracted a small gold mirror and a lipstick. "You are responsible for this." She pursed her lips and painted the top one brilliant red. "You must retrieve him." Examining her reflection appraisingly, she pressed her lips together and touched them with the tip of a scarlet fingernail. I couldn't decide who I'd strangle first after darkness set in: Natalie or Z.

Friends who later saw *Soul to Soul*, the film MGM made of the concert, say they caught a glimpse of me high up in a film crew tower. They tell me the music was wonderful. The crowd, they report, thoroughly enjoyed itself. My friends say everyone danced vigorously and, in between professional acts, dozens of small bands formed and performed. My friends obviously have a clearer picture of the festival than I do. I hadn't slept for forty-eight hours prior to being thrust into that fantastic scene of revelry, and much of the concert is a blur to me now.

I do remember the monotonous, eerie beat of African music contrasting with the familiar words and rhythms sung and played by the Americans. I remember being mesmerized by the sheer number of black faces illuminated in the firelight; a sea of blackness undulating in a black night. I have a flash of memory of eating something warm and filling from a wooden bowl an African woman handed me. I believe she wore a bolt of orange and purple tie-dyed cloth wrapped sari style around her body, but I may be mistaken about that. I do know that she guided me over to a circle of people gathered around a man whose sweat literally poured off his brow and on to the ground. His hands moved so swiftly over the top of a tall drum that they actually blurred in my vision. I remember trying not to stare, but staring anyhow in fascination at the tribal scars imprinted on some of the faces around me. My most vivid memories are, however, of smells. The pungent smell of rice and sauce and cook fires. The sour smell of sweat and clothes slept in for two days. The cloying smell of hibiscus and bougainvillea. The acrid smell of sewage and urine. And the all-pervasive, almost electric smell of dancing and singing and joyousness.

I have no recollection of how I ended up on the filming tower; I can only surmise that Natalie had met one of the crew and he'd invited us up there. I do recall her reappearing about that time. It was very far into the night by then, and I was utterly exhausted. Someone—a man with long, dark hair tied back in a ponytail—said he was going back to the hotel, and I remember grabbing him before he left and asking if there was an empty bed where I could take a nap.

We climbed down the scaffolding, sidled our way through the still celebrating crowd, and bounced in an open vehicle along suddenly silent dirt roads to a modern building. My benefactor slipped me a key and, although I was almost too tired to see, I managed to read the number on it and find the room.

When I regained consciousness on Sunday morning, the sun was just rising and the hotel door was moving inward. My eyes flew open and I sat straight up. "Um. Hi."

"Hello." He was surprised to see me there.

"I'm sorry. I guess I'm in your bed."

"Actually, yes."

I stumbled to my feet and attempted to straighten my clothes. "Someone—I don't know his name—gave me the key. We hitchhiked from Abidjan and it took two days and we didn't get to sleep much. Uh, you look pretty tired yourself. Have you been up all night?" While I babbled this nonsense, I was trying to gather my possessions that lay scattered on the floor.

"Um, yes."

"Well, thanks. For the use of your bed, I mean." I hastily tied the straps of my sandals. "It was great. It saved my life." I flung my backpack over one shoulder and stuffed my sleeping bag under the other arm. "I gotta go now. Thanks a whole lot."

His eyes were glazed as he stepped back slightly and held the door for me to pass through.

"Thanks again." I scurried into the hall. "Bye now." Flicking my fingers in a little wave, I watched the door close behind me.

Wait'll I tell Z and Natalie, I thought, forgetting my annoyance with them. Wait'll they hear that I slept in Carlos Santana's bed.

"Look, Natalie," I said, firmly. "We're gonna have to go without him. I start my new job tomorrow and I'm not about to miss the first day of work. You can either come with me or stick around and look for Z. I'm leaving now."

I'd found Natalie in the lobby of the hotel—she, too, had been offered a bed to rest in, although I didn't inquire whether it had been an empty one—and we'd returned to the festival to look for Z. He was nowhere to be found. Natalie was determined we needed a man to protect us on the return trip, and I was determined I was leaving immediately. For about an hour, we'd been debating the point. It was not yet noon, but from the position of the sun and the intensity of the heat I could tell it was close.

Since the hitchhiking idea had been a less-than-complete success, I'd plotted a different route for the trip home. Earlier that morning, while wandering through the crowd in search of Z, I'd struck up a conversation with the drummer I'd watched the night before. When I asked his advice about getting back to Abidjan, he suggested we take a bush taxi from Accra to a small village on the edge of a lagoon that formed a border between Ghana and the Ivory Coast. Although he'd never actually crossed the lagoon himself, he assured me that if we arrived an hour or so before sundown we'd be in time to catch the ferry. My advisor wasn't certain what kind of transportation awaited us on the Ivorian side of the lagoon, but we did already know what kind of transportation awaited us the way we'd come. One vehicle a day. So, in spite of the uncertainty, this seemed the better solution.

"Coming?" I flipped my backpack on and marched reso-
lutely in the direction of the taxi station.

"*Merde!*" S---! Natalie stamped her foot. "Wait up!"

Incredibly, everything went according to plan, at least at the
beginning. Natalie and I purchased the last two seats in the
bush taxi destined for the small village, whose name I have forgotten. The ride passed uneventfully which, as I was to learn
from later travels, is an event in itself. As we bounced along
gravel roads that gradually narrowed and turned to dirt, I
dozed fitfully. Natalie amused herself, and the three other
female occupants of the ancient station wagon, by carefully
reapplying her own makeup under their studious examination,
then painting their fingernails the same brilliant scarlet as
her own.

Four hours later, amid giggles and wishes for good luck and
prosperity, we took leave of our traveling companions. The
lagoon stretched out in front of us, a murky brown expanse of
motionless water. We could faintly see the far shore shimmering
greenly in the heavy afternoon heat. The ferry, which was actually more of a large wooden raft than a boat, was tied to two
posts at the end of a rickety wooden dock. It was absolutely
jam-packed.

"Why are there so many people?" I asked the one other bush
taxi passenger who was going aboard.

"They go to work in the Ivory Coast," he answered in oddly
accented British English. "Tomorrow is Monday, don't you
know?"

Stepping carefully across the dock so as to avoid gaping
holes where planks had rotted, we approached the boat. The
din was dreadful. Families called last minute instructions and
goodbyes to departing passengers, babies howled, hawkers
yelled descriptions of their wares, tinny music blasted from
portable radios, a horn boomed loudly and two huge men
wielding long boat poles shouted, "Move on. Move on," as they
untied the ferry's fraying ropes. Our companion thrust us forward and jumped aboard himself just as the boat eased slowly
from the dock.

"I can't believe this thing is seaworthy," I muttered, grimly.

Natalie moaned softly.

"And the lagoon is full of alligators," a familiar American voice said cheerfully.

Oh, good. We'd found Z.

Seemingly undisturbed by the close conditions, the passengers laughed and ate and gossiped as the ferry lurched out into the lagoon. Because we'd been the last ones on, we were at the edge of the boat, pushed up against the low rail. I gazed back at the dock. The families and hawkers and well-wishers left behind seemed to have settled in for a party. Momentarily, I forgot the mass of humanity pressing against me. I was in this wonderfully exotic world alone. Africa, I thought with a sudden rush of joy. I'm really here.

Screams alerted me to some new excitement, and then I felt the boat rock savagely.

"Oh, *Dieu!*" Natalie wailed.

"We're sinking!" Z's voice was high and ragged. "Jump off or we'll be crushed!" Even as he yelled at us, water poured in over the ferry's rim and the crowd behind swelled into something huge, inflated, and terrifying.

Unhesitatingly, I stepped up on the railing and flung myself overboard. My arms pulled me into a fast crawl and I swam several strokes from the sinking vessel before I stopped to look back. Z and Natalie were right beside me, but they were the only ones. The rest of the passengers moved as one large, panic-stricken body with innumerable limbs. The boat was barely visible.

"Jesus," I gasped. "They'll all drown."

It sounded like hell. Shrieks and lamentations coming from the water were echoed by the watchers on shore, many of whom were leaping into the lagoon and ineffectually striding toward us.

"*Ils ne savent pas nager!*" Natalie shouted, twisting her body to turn back to the sinking ferry. "They can't swim!"

It is a miracle that no one drowned that afternoon. Fortunately, we were only meters from water shallow enough to stand in, and Natalie, Z, and I were actually not the only swimmers. For the first time in my life, I understood the expression, "It seemed like hours. . . ." We grabbed bodies, struggled with them, screamed at them, and manhandled them to drag them the short distance to safety. By the time everyone was ashore, faint blue patches were visible all over my skin. The next day, I was covered with red welts and purple bruises from flailing arms and legs and elbows. According to Z's watch, the rescue had taken less than thirty minutes.

The fire glowed and humming voices throbbed. I was replete with chicken butchered in our honor, rice and sauce, palm wine and its lethal distillation, *koutikou*. With the ferry six leagues under, I had no idea how we'd get to Abidjan the next day or even the day after. At the moment, I really didn't care. In spite of my weariness, my aching body, and the headache I knew I'd have the following morning, I felt a curious peace. My eyelids flickered. A blurry vision through the fire made me smile. Z sat across from me, very erect, nodding slowly in agreement as one of the village elders spoke to him. Natalie's head was in his lap and, as she slept, he carefully smoothed her tousled hair.

The Field Librarian

Boma B. Obi

Collecting oral evidence from the Igbo villages in Imo State, Nigeria, near Lowa in Etiti local government areas, is not an easy task. It is better done during the rainy season so that one can meet the people at home, since farm work would have stopped. I planned my journey during the rains, and went to Lowa unannounced in order to forestall any attempt to withhold or adulterate information for collection.

On this drizzling evening, I set off for a certain compound where an old man dubbed "Papa" lived. He is reputed for his inexhaustible repertoire, and is properly equipped with oral traditions and their narration. When I got there, after exchanging the normal greetings and pleasantries, which are usually a bit on the lengthy side, I introduced myself and was given a seat. Next I fished out my reporter's notebook, turned on my tape recorder, and started an informal interview with Papa, who was seated in his easy chair in a corner in his living room.

I started by asking him when he was born. His reply was that he did not know exactly when, since reading and writing were not popular in the area then. He went on and mentioned a few names of other old men in the village who he said were his age mates. One of the men he mentioned claims to be about seventy-nine years old. The interview progressed. When Papa noticed that I was jotting things down in my notebook and also adjusting the tape recorder now and again, he stood up from

Ms. Obi is a librarian currently working as the Head of Serials/Reference Department of the Rivers State College of Education, Port Harcourt, Nigeria. She enjoys reading and writing, and is happily married with four children.

the easy chair with an agility I would never have dreamed he had. He asked me what I thought I was doing, then added, "Wait a minute, are you putting my voice in the radio?" I answered affirmatively. He then called one boy I suspected to be his son, whispered something to him, and in a flashlike movement, the boy disappeared. Meanwhile the interview stopped, because Papa had put on an uncompromising countenance. My thoughts went wild. So many things came to my mind as to what might have caused this sudden change of mind and vexation from the old man. Had I spoken insultingly, were my questions too personal? Had I been rude? The answer to them all was "no." I had been very courteous and cautious all along.

These questions were going through my mind when the boy reappeared. With him were five elderly men wearing serious looks. I greeted them, but received no greeting from any one of them.

My host then stood up and introduced me to the men as a government official from headquarters who had come to ask the secrets of the village. For her witness she has a radio into which she was putting his voice. He finished thus: "*Umunnam* [clan brothers], I have called you to come and witness what is taking me to prison and how I shall go there, so that you have firsthand information on what to tell our children and our children's children about my exit from the village. The saying of our elders that a man could remain in his home and yet trouble finds its way to him is a reality."

After the strange introduction, the elders busied themselves studying my face and looking at my jeans trousers. The latter they did with disapproval in their eyes. I was not shaken because I knew what I came for, and I was not a government official. To add to my composure I was there as one of them, being married to one of their kinsmen from the very next village. Still nobody spoke. They were just peering into my face and eyeing my jeans. The silence became uncomfortable, so I pressed on the tape recorder and tried to resume the interview in spite of the presence of our new friends. This time my question was "Papa, how did this village originate? Have you people always been here?" To this question, Papa, turning to his kinsmen with both hands spread towards them, replied: "Did I not tell you, she is a government official, that she wants to find out the secrets of this village? Never!" Turning to me he said, "My daughter, go back, go and tell those who sent you that you have not found us, eeh!"

At this point, all the men spoke nearly at the same time, each asking me to tell them who I really was and why I had come with a radio and a book to take statements. I tried to introduce myself. "I am a field librarian collecting and recording information about our villages for preservation in the library for posterity. This means that, when you honored and famous old men shall have lived as long as God wants you to, and gone back to Him [I did not want to mention death so as to avoid another misconception], we, your children, and your children's children, would always know from you through these records and the tape, what used to happen in the past. We would be able to hear your voices again."

I also added that I am the wife of Chief M. Obi's son. They all knew my father-in-law very well. One of them confessed that he had been looking at me since (as if that helped matters). It was after that that they all agreed to Papa granting me audience and answering my questions well. Singly and unnoticed, the five men left us.

The interview continued pleasantly with Papa and ended well. I felt quite happy because I collected a lot from him, including some oral poetry. After looking through my notebook to dot my "i's" and cross my "t's" I put it away and then pressed on the tape recorder to hear how the interview had been recorded. Papa listened to his voice with pride. He urgently sent for his wife and his relations from the inner part of the compound. They rushed in, and I increased the volume of the tape recorder. They listened with admiration and congratulated Papa. His wife, aged about fifty-five years, told him that she had always been sure he would go places in his life. Papa then asked me exactly where I was taking the tapes. I answered that I was taking them to the University of Ibadan (one of the best and most popular universities in Nigeria). Upon hearing this, Papa's wife let out an ululation of joy in which the entire household joined. When the excitement died down, I stopped the tape recorder, greeted them, and left for my own village, which is a long walking distance from where I went for the oral interview, and where I was going to spend the night before going back to Ibadan.

At home, the next morning, I was still in bed when I heard "knock, knock, knock" on my own door inside the compound. I had no guess who the caller could be at 5:30 A.M. My father-in-law is an early riser but he does not like to rouse people from sleep, especially "the book people" as he calls university graduates. The members of his family had learned that too. I tried not to get up, yet the knock came again. Curiosity got the better part of me and I got up. When I opened the door, lo and behold! It was Papa. I was too confused to say *"Anwuna* Papa."* Beaming with smiles he asked: "My daughter, is that thing still talking?" "Yes, Papa," I said. "It will continue to talk when asked to, even at Ibadan." "God bless you, my child," he said and left.

---

*Anwuna is the greeting of the area. It literally means "do not die . . ."

A Drop in the Bucket

Peter Spain

We were off the beaten path in Gambia that day, visiting remote village chiefs to maintain our visibility and garner their support for our evaluation of a health education project. The path we were on was simply a dusty track, traveled only occasionally by bush taxis and motorbikes—probably never before by a four-wheel-drive, bright blue American-made beast like our project vehicle. The fields along the path were mostly scrub and some peanuts. Stumps stuck up from fields like gravestones, markers of the devastation of local woodlands as well as of the poverty and density of the local population.

It had not been a particularly discouraging day. Indeed, the hospitality of the villages and of their chiefs was uniformly cordial; we had been assured by our local associates that we would be welcomed, as long as we followed a set of protocols that custom demanded when entering a village and seeking to talk with a chief. Having done this, we had been treated warmly, even lavishly in some places, where gifts of fruit and eggs and peanuts were thrust upon us. But, as a foreigner, one wonders, especially when following elaborate protocols, if the chief and his people really understand the substance of what you are about. While no discouraging words had been spoken this day —quite to the contrary—the questions remained: What do these folks really think of our work? Do they know about it? Are we

Peter Spain, Ph.D., has researched on village people and their response to communication programs in Mexico, the Philippines, and Gambia. He is currently a senior program officer at the Academy for Educational Development, Washington, D.C.

getting through? Have we contributed something? Do they find the project useful?

I was subdued in the face of poverty, and with the realization that poverty would be the lot of these people for a long time. Our project, while it could improve the health of some children, was a proverbial drop in the bucket. Even then I wasn't sure; was our drop actually reaching the bucket? These lingering questions, the bumps in the road, the dryness of the landscape, the broken trees, doubts about whether we would find shelter for the night, worries that the car would break down like last time—there were many reasons to be subdued.

Then, coming around a bend, we could see quite far ahead, and in one corner of a distant field was a line of women hoeing peanuts. We could see too that they had noticed us, because some had dropped their hoes. Then they started walking, running, toward the side of the field where our vehicle would soon pass. I had read that the president would be visiting the district the same week. Did these women think we were he?

As we came closer the women lined the side of the road, singing, clapping their hands, some dancing exuberantly, others waving with their hoes like undisciplined majorettes. Clearly they knew we were not the president. From the first moment we came around the bend they had recognized our unmistakable bright blue beast/vehicle. They wanted to cheer our project!

As we passed slowly, they shouted. It was like a ticker tape parade. While this wasn't exactly a ticker tape event, and the number of women not much of a crowd either, their enthusiasm was genuine and spontaneous. We waved back smiling, and continued our passage through the bush.

It was wonderfully affirming. Though the road remained bumpy and the landscape bleak, we felt far less subdued, and considerably more confident that our drop was indeed making a splash in the bucket.

Moussa's Table

Mary Louise Clifford

Once I built a table, a very primitive and slightly rickety table. The top was one end of a packing case in which our personal effects had been shipped to Africa. The legs were slats from one side of the packing case, cross-braced with more slats. The nails were salvaged from the same packing case. The hammer had been included in the household effects inside the box. This utilitarian table was needed because the laundry tubs were located in a walled enclosure outside the kitchen door. There was no place to fold the laundry when the houseboy took it down.

Our canny African cook leaned against the kitchen door jamb, hands in his pockets, and watched me build the table. When it was finished and set in place beside the laundry tubs, he admired it and announced that he would very much like to have such a table for his home.

The other half of the packing case, identical to the parts I had just dismantled, sat propped against the wall. *"Très bien, Moussa,"* I replied. Very good. "You may have the rest of the box. It has all the pieces you need. *Regardez.* Look. The top, the slats for the legs and cross-braces. The nails are all there in the wood. Here is the hammer. Bring it back when you have finished your table." I went into the house, feeling like lady bountiful.

A few days later Moussa returned the hammer, and I asked him how his table had turned out. He turned a slightly superior

Mary Louise Clifford has lived for extensive periods of time in several Third World countries and has written ten books (both fiction and nonfiction) for high school and middle school readers.

smile in my direction. *"Très bien*, Madame. The carpenter did an excellent job."

It took me several seconds to recover from my surprise. Moussa earned twenty-eight dollars a month; his fringe benefits included food, uniforms, and a bicycle. The French resented our being so generous to our servants and ruining the market.

"You paid a carpenter to build your table?"

"Oui, Madame."

"Moussa, I built our table," pointing to the modest piece of furniture in the dooryard, "and showed you how."

"Oui, Madame. But you are a woman."

Now I was really speechless. Finally, I collected my thoughts and counterattacked. "If my *monsieur* were not busy with his work at the *presidence,* he could have built the table."

Moussa sniffed. *"Ah, oui. Mais il est américain."* Yes, but he is an American.

I took a very slow breath, but kept my temper because I knew that deep-seated tradition ruled Moussa's life. "An American can build a table, but you cannot?" I asked gently.

"Madame," Moussa drew himself fully erect—all five feet four inches of him. "I am a cook. I am not a carpenter. Cooks do not build tables."

And, having set me straight, he went into the kitchen to tend to dinner.

A Gambian Coup

Mark Rasmuson

T*hursday, July 30.* As we are about to drive to the airport to welcome our new colleague from Stanford, arriving with his family from the States this morning, an American friend rushes up to our door and, seeing our ignorance, says: "You haven't heard? Turn on the radio. The airport's closed. Nobody's coming in or going out. There's been a coup."

We turn on our radio, and from Radio Gambia, with whom we have been making plans for the last two months to conduct a national radio health education campaign, gushes a stream of revolutionary rhetoric: "Long live the revolution! Long live the Supreme Revolutionary Council! Death to the corrupt and nepotistic regime of Jawara!" We are incredulous.

A few minutes later, one of the U.S. Agency for International Development (USAID) staff drives up to tell us to sit tight but keep in touch with the USAID director, who lives just a few blocks from us in the same suburb, Fajara, of Gambia's capitol, Banjul. He tells us to conserve the gas we have in our two project vehicles, and suggests we fill up our bathtub and buckets with water in case there is a service outage. Still mostly unconcerned and even entertained at the idea of a coup in this tiny, peaceful African country, we spend the next four hours listening to the radio. For the most part, it is the same recorded Marxist litany hour after hour, interspersed with warnings that looters will be shot on sight. But we also learn that the coup,

Mark Rasmuson is currently a resident advisor for the HEALTHCOM Project in Indonesia. Previously, he directed the HEALTHCOM Project in Washington. He has worked and traveled extensively in Africa and Asia.

staged while Gambia's President Jawara is attending the royal wedding in London, has the backing of Gambia's army, the 500-man Field Force.

We hear a few sporadic gunshots and the sounds of a crowd in the distance. I venture out once to try to buy gas, but am told that the Field Force has told all gas stations to sell gas to no one. Back at home, we pack up an overnight bag each, just in case.

At 2:00 P.M., we drive to the USAID director's and find an air of urgency and disturbing news: The rebels have freed and armed the prisoners in Gambia's one prison near Banjul; looting is extensive in Banjul and at the beachside hotels on the road towards us; a Canadian neighbor has been stopped by the Field Force, who put a gun to his head and forced him to his knees before commandeering his car. We are told to go home, lock our house, pack for a week, and bring our vehicles to the ambassador's as quickly as possible. The ambassador's house, a large mansion overlooking one of Gambia's most beautiful beaches, has been chosen as the refuge for the Americans in our neighborhood, though the ambassador himself and his staff are sequestered in the embassy in Banjul.

Now genuinely frightened, we rush home, lock up, throw our bags into the cars, and drive both through back roads to the ambassador's, only minutes away. We never imagine we will spend the next eight days there.

By 7:00 P.M., some ninety people have arrived at the ambassador's, some with only the clothes on their backs, others having emptied their houses of valuables and, luckily for us, food. Over the next few days, the number of refugees, who include, in addition to Americans, Canadians, French, Italians, Indians, Gambians, and Sénégalese, will reach one hundred twenty five, including twenty-five children, four dogs, and three horses.

We spend the evening sharing our stories, rumors, relief, and disbelief, and listening to radio messages over the ham set in the ambassador's bedroom, which a Peace Corps volunteer who is an experienced radio operator is monitoring. We are in touch with the ambassador in the embassy in Banjul, the British high commissioner, just a half mile away in another house overlooking the beach, and the American embassy in Dakar, to which we are transmitting the names of everyone here.

Early in the evening, we get a cryptic message from the British high commission that there is expected to be some "action" in the night. Shortly after, the first of several Séné-galese army planes are seen flying down the coast towards us.

People stake out sleeping space—the beds don't go very far—and by 11:00 P.M. practically every foot of floor space in the Ambassador's house is occupied.

Friday, July 31. We begin to organize ourselves. A food committee is appointed, and the Peace Corps organizes a system of watches: sentries (without arms, of which we have only one, a hunting rifle) at the front gate, on both sides of the house, and overlooking the beach below. They are very quickly reporting a constant stream of trucks and other vehicles on the road in front of the ambassador's. These vehicles carry loads of unarmed men in the direction of the Field Force depot, less than a mile away, and return a short time later carrying the same passengers and now bristling with rifles, headed past us in the direction of the airport.

On the other side of the house, looking out to sea, three ships are seen steaming south along the coast. They are too far away to identify positively, but we assume that they are Sénégalese troop carriers.

On BBC and Radio Sénégal, we hear President Jawara being interviewed in London and later in Dakar. He has invoked the Mutual Security Pact that Sénégal and Gambia signed in 1965, and has requested the intervention of Sénégalese troops. He claims that Sénégalese forces, parachuted in during the night, have already seized control of the airport.

Our sentries report that three truckloads of armed men have driven directly past the ambassador's house and appear to have stopped just two houses away, at the residence of the Séné-galese high commissioner. Immediately, everyone is ordered into the house and onto the floor of one of the bedrooms. All doors are locked and windows shuttered, and mattresses are piled against the windows of our "radio room." We are all sitting huddled on the floor of the bedroom, our silence broken only by the crying of several small children and occasional nervous laughter. I have never had a stronger or more frightening sense of life about to imitate art—cinema—those inevitable scenes from how many war movies where the enemy soldiers break into the last refuge and spray the innocent with bullets.

We don't have to wait long. There are several loud bursts of automatic weapons fire very nearby. Then all is quiet. A few minutes later, our sentries burst in to tell us that the three trucks and their passengers have driven away.

An hour later, we learn from Radio Gambia that the Sénégalese high commissioner and his family have been taken hostage, and that they will be killed if the Sénégalese have not been ordered to withdraw by 5:00 that afternoon.

This is the first of an extraordinary series of broadcasts from the rebel held Radio Gambia this afternoon. A short time later, the insurgents broadcast appeals to Guinea-Bissau, Guinea-Conakry, and the Soviet Union for assistance in resisting Sénégal's "invasion" of Gambia. Next there is a live, on-the-air negotiation session between the rebel leader, Kukoi Samba Sanyang, his Sénégalese hostage, and one of the Sénégalese military commanders. This results in nothing more than exceptional radio drama, as Sanyang tries to convince the Sénégalese officer to assist the rebels, while he insists that his troops are only here to restore law and order, and the Sénégalese high commissioner argues that he is not a hostage but a negotiator!

Finally, later in the afternoon, we are shocked to hear the anguished voices of one of President Jawara's two wives and her children on the air. Taken hostage earlier in the day, they are forced to plead with their husband and father to send back the Sénégalese troops. If he doesn't, they too will be killed.

Another scare: Our radio operator gets a message from the British high commission that several armed Field Force soldiers are on their way to us to use our radio to negotiate with Dakar. Only now do we realize what a precarious position we are in if it is known we are communicating directly with Dakar. Again, we huddle inside and again are relieved only a few minutes later: our spokesman has met the soldiers at the front gate and convinced them we have no direct radio link with Dakar, only to our embassy in Banjul.

This same scene—shuttering ourselves inside at the sound or the approach of armed men—is repeated a number of times over the next few days, but never are we directly attacked or threatened. While the insurgents take food and vehicles from the beach hotels nearby us, they in no way violate the diplomatic immunity of the ambassador's compound and are always very courteous in their encounters with us. Nonetheless, we are prepared to meet any demand they make of us, to the extent that we leave the keys in the ignition of all twenty-six vehicles in our compound so that the rebels will have no trouble taking them if they decide to!

Tonight, Laurel and I have volunteered to take the 11:00–12:00 P.M. shift of the night watch. As we sit on the front lawn in the pitch black, we are treated to a fireworks show—volleys of streaking red tracer bullets every few minutes from the rifles, we suspect, of nervous new rebels—almost as good as the one the ambassador threw at his Fourth of July picnic earlier this month.

Saturday, August 1. More organization, demanded by the alarming discovery that the water has gone off. A water committee is organized to assess our supply—a well that is discovered nearby—and we get a lesson from one of the Peace Corps volunteers in how to take a bucket bath. Volunteers also dig two latrines in the ambassador's back yard, since without water, flushing toilets has also become a problem.

Fortunately, both water and electricity stay on except for several short intervals during the week, and we remain for the most part well-cooled, well-washed, and cleanly dressed. In many other ways as well we are in a most commodious refuge: the ambassador has a good supply of magazines, paperbacks, and puzzles, as well as a horseshoe pit and a videotape machine on which we watch "Return of the Pink Panther" and "Chimps of The Gambia." Others have brought scrabble games, and chess and backgammon boards. The children, several of whom are younger than two years, and the dogs remain remarkably good humored. Our food supply is regular—two meals a day contributed from the freezers of a few veteran USAID types to whom this is all old hat. It is, however, neither exciting—oatmeal every morning—nor abundant. I lose eight pounds in eight days.

Today, all is quiet outside, though the traffic of armed insurgent vehicles on the road in front continues. We take turns keeping watch and wondering about the reports and rumors filtering in:

- The Soviets are implicated. BBC reports that arms and ammunition were smuggled in to the rebels in a shipment of sixty Russian Lada cars that arrived in Banjul the day before the coup. Rumor also has it that the rebel leader, Sanyang, of whom little more is known than his being a twenty-eight-year old failed candidate for Parliament in the last election, spent several years studying in Russia.

- The Libyans, kicked out of Gambia last year for forcibly impressing Gambian students in Libya into military service, are reported ready to intervene on behalf of the insurgents.
- The Sénégalese troops are reported to have moved halfway down the road from the airport to Banjul and to have taken Radio Gambia, which has been silent for the last twenty-four hours. But then, at 4:00 P.M., the rebels return to the air and claim to have taken more hostages.
- We are told that the U.S. State Department has set up a crisis desk in Washington, and has begun to consider our evacuation.

In the middle of the afternoon, a group of about ten Indian merchants are dropped off at our front gate by members of the Field Force. Proprietors of Chellaram's, one of Banjul's largest stores, they tell of two days of terror in the apartments above their store where they were held at gunpoint while every bit of their personal property was methodically looted. According to them, Banjul is still a battlefield, where a small number of loyal Field Force troops and police are holding out against the rebels from the barricaded police station in the center of town. The American embassy is just two blocks from the police station.

Later, another cryptic message comes over our radio, this time from the ambassador in the embassy: several "visitors" have arrived at the embassy. While pointedly not identifying who the visitors are, the ambassador asks us to begin transmitting coded messages, presumably from them, to Dakar, as the embassy's own radio link with Dakar has temporarily been lost. To our chagrin, we are expelled from the radio room from this point on, left to our wild speculations about who the visitors are. We learn only much later that they were indeed high Gambian officials.

Sunday, August 2–Tuesday, August 4. At 7:30 A.M. Sunday morning, we receive another message from the ambassador: the Sénégalese army has arrived in Banjul by helicopter and is now in control of the city. He assures us that the Sénégalese know of our situation and have promised they will secure the Fajara area as soon as possible.

We spend the rest of the morning listening to another series of pathetic broadcasts from the rebel radio: the president's wife, Lady Chillel, and children are made to go back on the air again to plead for their lives and for the Sénégalese troops to be withdrawn. One after another, the children say a few words each, often breaking off in tears: they are hungry and sick, confined to a single closed room, and afraid they are going to be killed. We are horrified at this cruel drama, which everyone feels must alienate whatever sympathy may remain for the insurgents' cause.

President Jawara, still in Dakar, goes on Radio Sénégal and says that the rebellion of these "ridiculous and sadistic buffoons" has been crushed. He declares a state of emergency and appeals for international relief assistance to deal with the aftermath of the crisis. He never does make any reference to the plight of his wife and children.

The rest of the next three days we wait for the Sénégalese army to arrive with both impatience and trepidation, for we know that ours will be a critical intersection of the fighting. The insurgents appear to be preparing to make a stand at the Field Force depot just minutes away, and have escorted many of the remaining expatriates in Fajara to the safety of several nearby hotels.

The insurgents go back on the air—we learn later that they have a mobile transmitter with which they successfully elude all Senegalese attempts to jam their broadcasts—to dispute Jawara's claims of control and to call again for popular support. While they repeat their threats about the hostages they hold, the several deadlines they have set for executing them pass without incident.

We learn that the ambassador has received a personal message from Secretary of State Haig to the effect that he is fully aware of and personally monitoring our situation. We are told that the status of planning for our evacuation has gone from red (hold) to yellow (get ready), and we organize accordingly: people repack their belongings into one or two manageable bags, and we are assigned to one of the twenty-six vehicles in the event that we must make a fast departure by land.

On Monday, our watchman-gardener Momadou appears at the gate of the ambassador's carrying a bag of papayas and bananas to us from our garden. He reports that the immediate area is still in the firm control of the insurgents, and that the markets are closed and food is in very short supply. We give him the key to our house with instructions to help himself to the food we have left behind, but to bring back one essential commodity for us. He slips away and returns an hour later to smuggle in our booty: two bottles of rum with which we had planned to celebrate the arrival of our Stanford colleagues and another equally important occasion. That night, with a few close friends, we sneak away with a potent rum punch to toast Laurel's thirtieth birthday and to forget—until we are rudely reminded the next morning—our captivity.

Wednesday, August 5. We are jolted awake at 7:00 A.M. by the hammer of automatic rifle fire just down the road. Everyone is on their feet instantly, piling mattresses against the windows again.

The Sénégalese have arrived in Fajara. Led by five armored vehicles, whose twin cannon fire makes the rebels' rifles sound like children's popguns, several hundred Sénégalese troops are moving down the road in front of the ambassador's, and at the intersection fifty yards away meet stiff resistance.

The fighting goes on all morning, but we have little idea of what is happening, as our sentries have been pulled inside, until our watchman Momadou appears at about 11:00 A.M., clearly very shaken. He had again been on his way to visit us early this morning when he was intercepted by the Sénégalese soldiers. Interrogated and held at gunpoint while the battle raged in front of him, he says that the bodies of Sénégalese soldiers, dead or wounded, are everywhere. He has also seen the house of the USAID director, where several rebels had run, riddled with cannon fire and grenade explosions.

By midafternoon, everyone has become so accustomed to the gunfire outside and unmindful of security that we are completely surprised when, at 4:00 P.M., there is a knock at the back door and in walks a cheerful British SAS commando, in civilian clothes but sporting an assortment of automatic hardware. Behind him, up the hill from the beach, come twenty-five to thirty Sénégalese soldiers in camouflage fatigues, lugging an assortment of rifles, machine guns, bandoliers of grenades and bullets, and two bazookas. Our liberators have arrived, and we treat them as such! Though the Americans have officially remained neutral throughout this conflict, we cluster around the sleek Senegalese soldiers like adoring children, and when one of their helicopters circles and lands on the beach a short time later, everyone is out on the back lawn cheering and waving wildly. To complete the scene of the liberating army, the soldiers even pass out chewing gum and chocolate from their French K rations to us!

Ten of the soldiers set up a perimeter around the ambassador's house. They will remain with us for the next two days, as the rest of their force moves down the road for the final confrontation at the Field Force depot.

Tonight, another happy surprise: our Peace Corps radio operator succeeds in connecting with another ham operator in Detroit, Michigan, who graciously offers to relay long distance telephone calls from us to as many of our homes as possible. From 9:00 P.M. to 3:00 in the morning, we take turns sitting at the radio talking across the miles and through the static to our families at home, thanks to this generous, anonymous soul. We all try to sound as reassuring as possible, but many of the hometown folks haven't the faintest notion of what is going on. How disappointing to learn that this vivid ordeal of ours and Gambia's is mere back page filler in the world's newspapers.

Thursday, August 6. A quiet, boring, frustrating day. The exhilaration over the arrival of the Sénégalese dissipates very quickly. Now that we know the immediate area is secure, we are all very anxious to be able to go back to our own homes—or at least down to the beach for a plunge in the surf. But we can do neither. We are ordered by the Sénégalese soldiers to stay put, until they have taken the Field Force depot down the road.

Late in the afternoon, we learn that they have done so with hardly a shot fired—the remaining rebels have fled into the bush. The rebellion is effectively over. More happy news: Lady Chillel, her children, and all the other hostages have been freed unharmed.

We learn later that the president's wife and children were rescued at the British Medical Research Council, where the rebels had taken them for treatment, by the same British commandos who led the Sénégalese to us. They reportedly had to do nothing more than walk, armed, into the MRC ward where Lady Chillel was being watched by unarmed guards. But for this violation of MRC's neutral no-arms zone, the SAS was roundly condemned by the MRC physicians, who accused their countrymen of behaving like louts and actually lodged a formal complaint with their foreign office.

We are still not allowed to go home. In fact, we learn that, after all, Washington has given the go-ahead to our official evacuation.

Friday, August 7. We are finally permitted to return home, but are instructed to come back to the ambassador's at 4:00 P.M. for further details of the evacuation. Many of us have strong reservations about the evacuation. We resent being arbitrarily designated "nonessential" personnel—certain "essential" embassy and USAID functionaries will remain behind—and question the wisdom of evacuating now, when we are seemingly out of danger. We also wonder about the impression on the Gambian people and government the evacuation will make, especially in the fashion proposed: a painfully visible mass exodus with Sénégalese military escort, first by motor convoy to the airport, then into a giant C-141 military transport bound for Dakar. We read later in a Sénégalese magazine that a Sénégalese army commander, piqued by the implied lack of confidence indicated by the expatriate's evacuation plans, had threatened to fire on any plane that tried to land at the airport for any reason in the early days of the rebellion.

Our minds are finally made up when we learn that we nonessential, nonofficial Americans will be charged first-class air fare plus $1.00 for the evacuation flight. We decide that we will drive to Dakar in our project vehicle, supply ourselves with food in the event that there are significant shortages in Banjul, and drive back—hopefully with our Stanford colleagues—as soon as the evacuation is called off. We luxuriate in a bed—our own—for the first time in eight days.

Sunday, August 8. After siphoning enough gas from several friends' cars to get us into Sénégal, we set out with two friends for Banjul, where we will catch the ferry across the Gambia River.

We expect to see visible evidence of the rebellion, and we are not disappointed. There are a number of bullet riddled or burned-out vehicles along the roads, which are heavily patrolled by the Sénégalese soldiers in tanks and trucks. In Banjul itself, the windows of many looted shops are boarded up, and one of the largest and oldest stores—Maurel and Prom, a French company that has been in West Africa for 150 years—has been completely gutted by fire. But Banjul is not the disaster zone we had been led to believe it was. Already most of the streets have been cleaned up, and people seem to be going about their business as usual.

At the ferry crossing, the Sénégalese are carefully checking the papers and body searching every Gambian boarding. We are passed through quickly, one of only three vehicles on the ferry, that usually packs fifteen to twenty autos and trucks on board. The passage across the wide expanse of the mouth of the river takes about thirty minutes, and affords me the first look at Banjul from the water that I have had since arriving two and a half months ago. Apart from the loud coming and going of Sénégalese army helicopters, its palm-lined shores appear as quiet and peaceful as Gambia has always been until recently.

Twenty minutes after disembarking on the other side of the river, we are at and through the border without incident and driving through the Sénégalese countryside, which differs from Gambia only in that the road signs are in French rather than English. Five hours later we are in Dakar—the Paris, some say (others, Marseilles), of Africa and our safe haven, from which we hope to return in only a few days.

Epilogue. Our stay in Dakar proved longer and less safe than we guessed. For reasons still unclear to us, as conditions appeared to normalize quickly in Gambia, we were required to stay in Dakar for eighteen days until the evacuation was officially called off by the ambassador in Banjul and approved in Washington. After being mercilessly harassed and hustled by the street people of Dakar, we were convinced we would have been much safer back in our homes in Gambia.

One advantage of our stay, however, was being able to read about the recent events in the city's French-language newspapers, which were filled with stories and photos of *les événements de gambie*, the Gambian incident. Along with the expected editorials lauding President Abdou Diouf's courageous intervention and felicitations from other African heads of state, the Sénégalese newspapers also reported much more straight news than the Gambian, which in the best of times report little of any news value and were now under the strictures of emergency powers. Here, in brief, is the view of the rebellion's aftermath we gleaned from *Le Soleil* and other Sénégalese periodicals, and from our own observations since returning to Gambia on August 26:

The aborted coup left between 500 and 1,000 dead. The government and people of Gambia were left in a state of shock—no one could believe such violence could occur here. President Jawara appealed for and has received millions in international relief aid, including an outright $10 million gift from Saudi Arabia. Many wonder why all this relief aid was necessary and where it will go, since there was no substantial disruption of the economy. Part of it is going to provide free rice to the entire Banjul area for ninety days, the first time in Gambia's history that such a distribution has occurred.

Presidents Jawara and Diouf have announced that there will be some kind of confederation between Sénégal and Gambia—the long awaited Sénégambia?—though how, what, and when still remain unclear. Everyone agrees that there will be a Sénégalese military presence in Gambia for some time to come.

The United States apologized to the Gambian government for any wrong impression that might have been given by the American evacuation.

Upwards of 700 persons, including a number of senior civil servants and the heads of the opposition party, have been detained under the emergency powers act and are appearing before a tribunal for their parts or suspected parts in the rebellion. The rebel leader, Kukoi Samba Sanyang, and nine of his followers escaped to Guinea-Bissau, where they were apprehended by the Bissau authorities early in August. As yet, however, they have not been returned to Gambia, and it is not clear what Guinea-Bissau proposes to do.

Jawara is reportedly reviewing long-standing reports of incompetence and corruption among his ministers, which are universally acknowledged and deplored by Gambians, but there has been no substantial reshuffling yet.

Our own department, Medical and Health, like many others, was badly shaken up. One of its brightest young doctors was shot while driving in an ambulance and lost his leg, and another prominent member of the department has been arrested and detained. We are slowly getting our own project back on track.

A Modern Doctor Schweitzer

Cesar A. Chelala

He has some physical features in common with Dr. Albert Schweitzer. He is tall, and has a moustache and an incipient beard. But, more significantly, he has the same obsession to help the suffering and the poor. Getting to know him revealed an idealism in the service of my profession I rarely see nowadays, and that is why I remember him so well.

I was visiting the continental half of Equatorial Guinea called Rio Muni with some medical colleagues to appraise the health situation in the country. We had arrived at Niefang, a small, sparsely populated, neglected town in the interior. The high humidity made the heat even more oppressive, typical of that region.

In the hospital I was introduced to Dr. Ramon Vila, a Spanish physician in his middle thirties. He was calm and self-assured, radiating warmth. When we arrived he was treating a difficult case, an adult man whose body was covered by large, irregularly shaped, infected ulcers. An unpleasant smell was present everywhere. Dr. Vila described the health status of the other patients in the ward, and then led us on a tour of the hospital.

He took us to the delivery room, shared with the first aid room—a fact that increased the possibilities for the spread of infections. Scarce financial resources, he explained, made this unavoidable. Everywhere throughout the hospital we saw

Dr. Cesar A. Chelala is an international medical consultant, and a co-winner of the 1979 Overseas Press Club of America award for the best article on human rights. He frequently writes on international affairs.

crowded facilities, poverty, lack of essential items, run-down services. Dr. Vila did not seem to be affected by these difficulties.

Afterwards, at his home, he told me, "We chose this country following a curious circumstance. I was studying with a colleague a rather unusual case, one of only 211 recorded in the medical literature. Suddenly, I was struck by the irrationality of my study. What was its purpose, I thought, when all over the world millions of men, women, and children are hungry and live in total misery? That is when I decided to go to Nicaragua where," he continued, "I learned to look at death in a new way. I found out that the Nicaraguans are a truly remarkable and stoic people. They have a profound sense of friendship, of love. However, if one of them is killed, they quietly bury the dead and continue their struggling life."

After spending time in Nicaragua, Dr. Vila and his wife went to Africa, where they had clearly developed a very special relationship with the people in the area. When I asked about his plans for the future, he told me, "I want to remain here. You see, there are times when one does things not because of the comfort they bring but for a different reason—a moral call if you wish. That is the challenge I found here. In Barcelona I would be irritated by a temporary lack of electricity, or by what I assume to be an unchanging red traffic light. Here I fight every day against death, and many times I am the loser in the battle. But here I feel fulfilled. I know that in this place, despite its primitive conditions, my work makes a difference. I wouldn't change that for anything in the world."

I felt humbled in his presence—as one must have felt in the company of the kind and gentle Schweitzer, in a different time and place that was nonetheless Africa.

Letters Home
I

Polly Stephens

Upon arriving, we were stopped once by an "immigration check," which appears to be quite common. Dr. Cole gave the "immigration officer" a coin and on we went. On our way up country Dr. Cole was recognized by someone at each of the three immigration checks we went through so the ride was free. Then I was taken to the Christian Health Association of Liberia (CHAL) and left to sleep in a woman's apartment as she was leaving for Zimbabwe. Unfortunately she recently acquired a water bed so I wobbled around all night. I awoke early and was ready to greet five beaming missionaries who had arrived on Tuesday and were waiting to go to Phebe Hospital. Fortunately, the pastor's wife taught me the Liberian handshake (shake hands and snap each other's third fingers at the end), which sounds easier than it is but I'm getting the hang of it. She suggested that I shake hands with everybody (apparently the kids love it) and just be careful about not putting my fingers in my mouth until I can wash my hands.

Later we did errands in Monrovia: got four pictures of me taken for the immigration office, then went to a man's house to give him everything so he could get the permit for me. He wasn't there so we decided to try to do it ourselves. We walked through the Barbershop Saloon doorway and upstairs to the entrance, which was locked. We knocked. People were on the other side but paid no attention. We waited. Dr. Cole is

Polly Stephens will receive her medical degree from Tulane University in June 1993. In between undergraduate school and medical school, she was a volunteer with a rural health program in Liberia.

extraordinarily patient and I have a feeling it's cultural. Finally a woman came up and suggested we try another entrance. Outside, past a man knocking a hole in a wall, around the corner, up the stairs, past some people in jail, into an office. I gave the woman my stuff, she stamped and signed, Dr. Cole gave her a coin, and we left. Then we went to visit a Lebanese shoe salesman who is also Dr. Cole's financial advisor or something. We had sodas, then left.

At the final destination a million little kids appeared and carried boxes into the house. The electricity had been out for a number of days. It got dark at 7:00 P.M. Dr. Cole and I sat in the dark for a while and then had bread and tea. My placemat had a picture of Independence Hall in Philadelphia on it. The curtains in this room are Winnie the Pooh theme, and Star Wars is in the bathroom. I had a bucket bath.

Final destination! I am in my house. It has four bedrooms! I am here all alone. It's on the top of a hill and has a great view. My bathroom is about 20 meters from the house. Half is a room to shower in, the other half is the toilet area. I think I will try to take care of all bathroom matters before I go to bed. It's dark now and pouring rain, which makes the prospect even worse. My household goods include a kerosene stove (one burner), sheet, pillow, pillow case, kerosene lamp, knife, fork, and spoon, one cooking pot, two glasses, and one water pot that filters water (my water comes from a deep well and then I filter it). The house is kind of furnished—beds, a dresser, kitchen table and wobbly chairs, and living room set. I have a bucket in which to put water to bathe in. I also bought some food today: tea, bread, bananas, crackers, jam, and cheese. So far the food has not been great. Rice is a staple, usually covered with a meat/vegetable dish. *Foo-foo* is a tribal food made of cassava and looks like a mass of clear jelly or dried opaque glue. To eat it you take a spoonful and dunk it in a thick soup and then swallow it without chewing—just swallow!!

Today I opened my door and a huge lizard fell on my head. I found a huge cockroach on my sneaker—they also frequent my outhouse. It's evening and the crickets are chirping louder than ever. Last night one of my neighbors came and offered to live here with me. I didn't really understand what was going on, so she spent the night. Today I talked it over with Mrs. Dr. Cole, who said it was perfectly all right if I stayed in the house by myself so I sent Kaipo home. She is in seventh grade, doesn't know how old she is, and is one of about fourteen kids of the same father—I'm not sure about the mother.

Letters Home
II

Raymond Downing
Jan Armstrong

Dear friends,

One thing is clear: no matter how long we stay in Africa, we will never become black. This simple truth may seem obvious to you, but we are reminded of it almost daily, whenever we walk or ride anywhere. Children are of course fascinated by people who look different, and when we walk or drive past them, they express their fascination by staring or pointing and chanting *"Kawaja! Kawaja!"* (white person or foreigner) while jumping up and down. Adults are a bit more subtle: they just stare and say *"Kawaja"*—without jumping up and down. Debbie, one of our coworkers, decided some time ago that an appropriate response might be to have little cards printed to hand out to all who greet us this way; cards that say, "Congratulations, you have correctly identified another *Kawaja*."

Since this *Kawaja* "greeting" is so common, and in fact can get quite irritating, we find that we employ different methods, or stages, of responding. One stage—an early one—is to try to greet everyone who calls us *Kawaja*, be flattered by the attention, and help them practice their English or use the opportunity to practice our Arabic. This stage lasts about one day. Sometime later, when the "greetings" continue and begin to sound more like "nigger" than "honored foreigner," the

---

Raymond Downing and Jan Armstrong, husband and wife, collaborate on the content of their submissions; Raymond writes them. Both are doctors who worked seven years in Appalachia, three years in the Sudan with the Mennonite Central Committee, and most recently in Tanzania doing both hospital and primary health care work.

aggravation builds a bit, and we find ourselves yelling back "Sudanese!" in response. This witty, mature comeback accomplishes precisely nothing. A third stage is the silent response, ignoring *"Kawaja"* greetings and saying to myself each time, "My name is not *Kawaja.*" This accomplishes two things: a blunted conversation, and guilt at lack of sociability. The most psychologically advanced stage we've discovered to date is direct confrontation: gently face the chanters and hoardes of kids following us and ask exactly why they're following and what they want. The success of this method matches the others: we asked a small group of kids once, "What do you want?" and a little boy responded with disarming honesty, "I want to look at you."

Fortunately, our many refugee and Sudanese friends do not call us Kawaja. In fact, since Elizabeth and Tim call us Mommy and Daddy, all the neighbor kids think these are our names—and so we are called Mommy and Daddy by fifteen kids.

About 4:30 one afternoon we walked across the way to Abraham and Nebyat's house uninvited. Abraham promptly found some chairs for us and we sat under the *racuba* (a grass shelter) outside his house—a round grass hut. Meanwhile his wife Nebyat began fanning the charcoal fire and getting out the raw coffee beans, the pan to roast them, and the flask-shaped coffee pot. Our children wandered off with their children, Timothy drifting back to us a bit more frequently than Elizabeth. Chickens pecked on what they could find under our chairs.

We talked quietly, easily. Abraham knows English better than we know Arabic or his tribal language; Nebyat understands some and mostly listened. Abraham is tall and thin, with a methodical mind and a boyish grin. Nebyat is small, quiet, and attractive; she has an Orthodox cross tattooed on her forehead. They both work in the clinic. They got their initial medical training "in the field," as medics in Eritrea's war for independence from Ethiopia; before that they were both guerrilla fighters. But Nebyat was too small to fight, and Abraham got wounded.

When Nebyat finished roasting the coffee beans she put them in a heavy wooden cup and pounded them with an iron rod until they were ground. During this time her six-month old baby clung tenaciously to her breast and nursed. She then put the grounds in water in the pot on the fire, boiled it three times, and served us in tiny porcelain cups.

As we drank two, three, eventually four of these little cups, each one quarter filled with sugar, we talked of resettlement. I could feel Abraham's ambivalence about wanting to go to America, but knowing his chances were small; of disliking Sudan, but beginning to realize it was his home. We asked what he heard from his friends who had gone to America, what they noticed as most different from Africa. He thought for a minute, then he answered simply, "Time is golden."

Time in North America and Europe is indeed as valuable as gold. We try not to waste time, we plan how best to use—or manage—it. We convert it into money, or results, or knowledge. We count it, and use it for what seems most important; but like money, we never seem to have enough of it. Time, to us, is in fact golden.

By 6:30 it was dark; Abraham had lit a kerosene lamp. We could see Orion and the Pleiades easily; we could see the Milky Way behind them with no city lights to compete. Time here is not golden. It's as plentiful as sheep and goats. It's treated as casually as trees, hacked down and not replaced, as if the supply of both was infinite. Progress and development require us to treat time as a valuable resource, to use it wisely, to redeem it. But then it becomes a commodity like money, and we cannot be as anxiety free as the lilies of the field, for we worry about not having enough. We mastered time and we progressed; now it masters us. In Africa time grows wild like the lilies of the field —and progress still eludes Africa. Time is but one reason why.

We, of course, still find ourselves treating time as golden, and consequently will have a busy schedule for the next few months with teaching and increased supervision in the wake of the coup here. Elizabeth and Timothy never think about time; they play with their many friends from dawn until dark.

CHAPTER 3

ASIA AND THE NEAR EAST

"Let Them Only Be Sleeping"

I n Bangladesh, a kind of claustrophobia envelops you as you walk the streets thick with human beings. The dense population becomes even more awesome when you suddenly realize that almost everyone in sight is male. Although bodies in the streets do not match legendary proportions, or even one's own mental image conjured up defensively in preparation, the poverty and deprivation are very real and clear. For me, this will be ever imprinted in my mind by the memory of a woman, no more than twenty, lying on the pavement with her infant child. "God," I thought, "let them only be sleeping."

—Elayne Clift

The Journal

Frances J. Connell

Tashkurghan, Afghanistan, September 1973–June 1975. Summer and the falling heat like an out-of-season coat. The baked faces of turbanned men who walked donkeys along the treeless road, stone-heavy burlap bags curved over their shoulders like hunchbacks. Boys with stick legs, and girls covered by full dresses like faded flowers sat on bare heels along the open ditches; and the women under ghostly veils passed by.

A solitary camel, armies of goats in black file, the nomad tents like overturned pots, piles of wound rope and stretched skins, and the land colorless, the color in the faces of the people. The *kutchie*—nomad—trucks, painted tin contraptions that fumed and snorted from north to south, their gaunt drivers crazed in the constant light, passing the houses whose walls held up the sky like an azure scarf.

The bazaars, clusters of mud huts and straw roofs arching over the shopkeepers, torn legs folded under layers of coats and capes and vests, backs stiff as meditators, motionless among the fruit and piled vegetables, silk and spun cotton, packaged Russian soap and round tins, bottles of dyed water, and the sourceless trinkets. On market days the strangers from the hills, toothless Turkoman farmers, their high bones gathering light as

Former Peace Corps volunteer and college teacher, Ms. Connell has had poems and stories published in a dozen small magazines, and is currently seeking publication of two novels. She lives with three sons and her husband in the middle of lots of trees in Silver Spring, Maryland.

the dust crawled across their hands, squatting around a load of dry brushwood, the stiff weeds gleaned from the desert to sell; for they burned the earth's hair.

The scent of livestock like a flash of light; the smell of waking babies, of damp leather and flayed animal flesh, of grass cloyed with ripe clover, of men moving under cloth ironed stiff from their sweat.

The sanctuary of old age, the teahouse on the edge of the walking world. The most ancient men knighted in white turbans, the scraggly beards a final stroke on their dark, lined faces; the loose clothes falling around them like colored clouds. Daily they sat beside the river and watched, while the thin tea, light as drying hay, boiled in the polished samovar; and from the chipped china bowls they sipped one portion for a morning.

The schools damp and undecorated. Rooms indistinguishable small blocks in daybreak, with triple rows of benches and short, warped desks; the tottering pitted blackboards, the screenless windows, and the children's eyes. A religious scholar with eyes as wild as melon seeds, bowing each morning beside the mosque as he came. Day's end the crickets wait for dusk. The mullah's cry and the final evening prayer, lonely as gathered time, the strains obliterating all sounds during its solo flight, the deposited daily coverlet of faith. And evening had put the sand to sleep.

At night the drumming of horses along the cobblestones and dirt streets, the scarred gardens fragrant with breezes from the understalks. Dogs chanting on walls, swallows from the niches in the hay-thatch roofs turning with dark into birds with leather wings; and the cool rising like spring dust. The watchmen who call from the marketplace when the stars stare blankly in their frozen sea, and the voices float up and over the village asleep, flickering like lanterns. Soldiers shout on the roofs, their echoes buckle like a trapped desert animal.

The way the fruit trees blew then, the little rivulets of wind, specter in a waterless land; and the desert stole over you, an edict. Then winter came, gray as duck down, with a sunless sky and a wind that scurried around the windows. In the morning the boys sold bread and yoghurt. Covered in stocking caps and too large jackets, nothing visible of their bodies, they stood in long lines holding their dishes on thin, tiered ropes like scales. And the little girls, still in the thin widow-weed school suits, walked by.

The winter walking the days, trucks faltering by, leaving men as strangers. Clusters of sheep climbing like scorched grass among the hard soil. The mountains sulkier, dark tempered with heavy clouds, until the snow came, lying first in the passes like fresh cotton. The winds swept in from the northern steppes, the scythelike wind cut the village, and lives behind cold mud walls adjusted themselves as they always had, or passed out. Under their blankets of rough wool, smoky with burning dung and thistles, they recounted again how the days would go by while the work slackened and got done, and the year counted out its old ways.

One day a warmer breeze, and all the boys rose with the first sun and went out of their houses to fly paper kites. All morning the frail birds tumbled and soared in the sky alone, and the children pulled them in to put them out again. A snake charmer gathered a crowd in the marketplace with his basket and coiled snake and elliptical flute, while a magician by the river promised to bring a plate of steaming rice out of his coat, and a lame man with a capped monkey set the creature dancing for a coin.

Until another season, spring, followed the long winter, rain to make the village turn to acres of mud. Unarmed against the pounding moisture, houses and schools and shops sprang leaks like wounds; and the village limped in the valley of brown blood. Until one day it dried and around everywhere were green fields of rice, wheat, and flowers, the blood red poppies, the yellow and pink violet desert stalks with names like a thogony; and the birds glided between the rocks edging each meadow like large, fragile butterflies. Then, it was no longer spring, but summer again, and another year had passed.

A Friend from
New Town Girls' School

Mary Louise Clifford

I met her first at a U.S. Information Service (USIS) open house. Safia Khan—a small, black-haired, dark-eyed woman in her early forties, moving gracefully in a pale green sari and making gentle conversation in her soft, precise English.

When I learned that she was the headmistress of a Pakistani girls' school, my antenna started quivering. I had no intention of spending my time in Karachi drinking coffee and playing bridge. I asked Safia to let me help at her school. Her eyes lit up, and she invited me to appear there on Tuesday at 10 A.M.

I arrived during recess. Two students in blue and white *shalwar kamiz* (a shirt and trouser uniform) rushed to open the iron gate in the high adobe wall surrounding the huge compound. I parked my station wagon in the shade of the thick banyan trees that lined the center drive and looked around me. Groups of girls, all wearing the same blue and white costume, were scattered across the wide space between me and the low building at the far end of the drive. Along the walls and among the flowering shrubs they sat in twos and threes, hunched over notebooks. Beyond the trees, games of volleyball and tag and kick-the-stone swept across the hard-packed brown earth. In the far corner a group of girls were cooking over a small brazier, and on a nearby table another group pasted scrapbooks. A few special

---

Mary Louise Clifford has lived for extensive periods of time in several Third World countries and has written ten books (both fiction and nonfiction) for high school and middle school readers.

friends strolled arm in arm under the huge trees, while near the drive three girls filled sprinkling cans from a spigot and watered the flower beds.

The two who had opened the gate for me waited while I got out of my car, then led me shyly up the steps of the school verandah and down a dark hall to Safia's office. It was the tiniest, least comfortable room in the building, the one that got the full force of the noon sun and the noise of the boys' school next door. Safia told me later that the students needed the best facilities far more than the headmistress. This also explained the fact that the narrow corridor leading to her office was the teachers' room, where they sat crammed so closely in the straight wooden chairs along the wall that you had to step carefully to avoid crushing someone's feet. The telephone hung in a small cubbyhole beyond a partial screen, ringing constantly amidst the noise and confusion of the tiny anteroom.

Safia introduced me down a line of limp handshakes and shy smiles. A few moments later the elderly school *ayah* (nurse) limped out on the long verandah and struck resounding notes with a wooden mallet on a huge brass gong. In every part of the compound, books, papers, balls, and tools were gathered quickly together, and four hundred and fifty girls trooped to form a tight mass around the steps. Morning assembly took place here every day following recess, because the school building contained no room large enough to hold more than one class. Here Safia gave out the day's instructions and announcements in her soft Urdu. Often one or another of the teachers spoke for a moment, and on some mornings there were special guests to be introduced.

I was totally unprepared when two shy teenagers stepped forward and welcomed me in careful English, asking me to come back to speak with them and teach them American folk songs. One brown-eyed nymph presented me with a bright bouquet of marigolds, while the other held out a daintily embroidered glasses case. As they stepped back, the expectant silence told me that they were waiting for me to respond. Safia should have warned me.

I looked at all those upturned faces as I thanked them for their welcome and their gifts, wondering, Could I make them smile? Respond to my questions? Ask me questions in return? Tell me of their hopes and aspirations? When the assembly was finished, I looked at Safia and thought, Oh, you clever woman —leaving it to your bright-eyed students to win my heart.

For many months after that I went back at recess time and watched the assembly from the shade of the big banyan tree. When it was finished, one group of girls would detach themselves from the mass flowing inside the building and come over under the tree to join me. They brought heavy cotton rugs to sit on, carefully removing their shoes and lining them up alongside. They brought a small frame blackboard on which I wrote song words while they settled themselves around my stool and copied the verses in their notebooks. Sometimes a teacher joined us, a silent reminder to the girls to pay strict attention. Sometimes another class was free that period and sent a delegation to ask if they might join the singing. Often this meant my semicircle contained seventy to eighty girls, but who could say no to such enthusiasm?

We started every session with "Good Morning to You," a nursery tune, but appropriate in its simplicity. The music these children knew is very different from Western harmonic music. They sang a scale of seven whole tones, with a pattern of a quarter tone between each. Nor is what they sang written down, but rather passed from person to person by memory. Their vocal music is traditionally for a single voice, with the solo performer having great latitude to make variations on the theme. Some of them volunteered that solo singing was their hobby, but the group singing that we enjoy in our homes and schools and churches is foreign to Pakistani children. They had no vast body of folk songs that are hummed and whistled and sung in chorus all over the land. They had no music classes in their school, and none of the girls played an instrument of any kind. In fact, some of their conservative Moslem parents felt that music and dance were frivolous and improper, and Safia took care in broadening her curriculum.

"Could I do some folk dancing as well?" I had asked.

"I'm not sure we're ready for that," she replied.

So we sat under a banyan tree and learned "Good Morning to You" and "Old Susannah" and "I've Been Working on the Railroad." The repertoire was determined by the rhythm and simplicity of melody. With no musical understanding, the girls could learn only those simple tunes that stayed in their heads. Their absolute favorite was a bouncy jingle in Urdu about the *tonga-wallah* (horse carriage driver), which has the joggy rhythm of the trotting horse. The chorus urged the horse to "Come on, hurry, hurry," and it was the one song, along with their national anthem, that even the youngest girls could sing without any help from me.

They loved rounds such as "Are You Sleeping?" although it took great concentration for the girls to ignore the counter verses. They were also very fond of "Johnny's So Long at the Fair." Many of my students tied their long brown braids with blue ribbons to match their blue shirts. The idea of Johnny bringing "a bunch of blue ribbons to tie up my bonny brown hair" made them giggle.

The Pakistani teacher had to translate explanations of some of the more difficult songs—"Yankee Doodle," "Skip to My Lou," "Jimmy Crack Corn"—for this was the sixth class, and they were just beginning their five years of secondary school English. Safia had chosen this youngest class to sing because they were the least self-conscious and most eager to throw themselves wholeheartedly into such monkeyshines. While I imitated them and pretended to sing with my mouth closed, they laughed uproariously, then gaily stretched their jaws as we all produced big round sounds. Singing with the older classes was less successful, in spite of their better command of English, for they were far more inhibited.

Safia knew what she wanted. "Expose the girls to some of the thoughts and ideas and pleasures that are important to you —awaken their interest in other peoples and other cultures."

"Have any of them known any Americans before?"

"No, that's why your coming is such a treat. They take their school opportunity very seriously. They need to see how humane you are. When they realize how much you enjoy singing, they will see that music is an integral part of making you, a foreigner, the person that you are."

This made my assignment pure joy. It mattered not how well the girls sang or how well I sang or that my singing was often cause for laughter. Mutual enjoyment was our goal. Of course, we did more than sing. Often the girls brought a handful of flowers for me from their home gardens. I fastened them in the straps of my accordion, talked about what they were called and how they were grown, and leaned over frequently to smell them. We discussed the planes flying overhead, the two kites (oversized crows) who perched in the limbs above our heads whenever we sang, and the various sounds that came in from the street. One day a most beautiful triplet of notes came floating over the wall. The girls knew it came from a small whistle made of a short split bamboo reed with a funnel-shaped horn of paper, gaily painted. One of them ran to buy one for me from the *wallah* (peddler) outside the wall; it cost three annas (about two cents) and used outdated pages of the American embassy news bulletin for its funnel. Mine blew only one note, rather than the lovely three that had caught our attention, and we laughed together as I experimented with its sound.

As the weeks went by, I began to know the students and their teachers as individuals, and to speculate about what kinds of homes and families they came from. Safia explained that the simple blue *kamiz* (long shirt) over white *shalwar* (full trouser) with white *duputta* (stole) thrown over the shoulders was chosen to make all the girls look alike and conceal the vast differences in their backgrounds. New Town Girls' School was one of the best private Moslem girls' schools in Karachi, and some of the students came from excellent homes. Others were less fortunate, some were scholarship students, and even the daughter of the school's elderly caretaker attended. The uniform served its purpose admirably, for it revealed very little about economic status. A shoe that needed reheeling might indicate poverty or simply an oversight. A torn *duputta* could result from an accident in the gym class that morning, and a neatly mended *kamiz* could indicate a thrifty mother in any station of life.

The one characteristic that was not concealed by the uniform was the degree of seclusion in which the girl lived. Some of them came from families that had already entered the modern world, but others were from very conservative, traditional backgrounds. I occasionally saw a girl slipping in the front gate, hastily stripping off her black *burqa* (robe) and bundling it under her arm.

"Why on earth are these girls still wearing those things?" I asked Safia. It seemed a contradiction when they were getting a good education.

"Oh, it's their parents who keep them in *purdah* (seclusion). They'll abandon the *burqa* when they finish school."

"I should hope so!"

One day, however, I learned firsthand how severely restrictive *purdah* can be. The high school girls at the American school were putting on a fashion show, and I suggested to Safia that some of her students and teachers might like to attend. We worked out the logistics to take a dozen girls and three teachers across town in my and another station wagon to see this entertainment. I did not realize when we arrived that the girls had bundled their *burqas* in the back of the other station wagon—where I wouldn't see them.

The driver of the other car went off during the performance and, it later turned out, couldn't remember how to get back to where he had left us. When the show and the refreshments were finished, the girls shyly confessed that they could not leave until the other car returned with their *burqas*. They couldn't walk home from school or take a taxi or a bus without their robes, for it was the men of the street from whom their parents kept them veiled.

We waited with growing impatience for the missing driver, then finally decided that I should take one teacher and as many girls as my station wagon would hold back across the city to the school compound, where we would try to track down the missing car.

One of my passengers asked to be let out at a bus stop. She said she was not in *purdah* and seemed quite confident that she could make her way home alone by bus. By now I was a little paranoid, but her teacher let her go. When we reached the school, the teacher phoned the residence where the lost driver worked and found him there. He did manage to return to the school with the missing *burqas*. Another American mother appeared shortly, transporting the girls who had been left behind with their two teachers, and, reunited with their *burqas*, they could then proceed home.

This straightening out had required a couple of extra hours and soured me a little on excursions. Not so the Pakistani girls; they repeated many times how great their enjoyment at seeing this novel entertainment. One of the teachers was just as touching. "I've never been to a foreign function before," she confided.

I enquired if they had minded the photographer, who had snapped pictures all over the place.

"We don't mind being photographed. It's our parents who mind."

One of the students asked shyly about the strapless evening gown. "What makes it stay up?"

"There are metal supports in the seams."

"Where would she wear it?"

Try explaining that to a young woman who would never be alone with a young man until she married him.

When the older girls proved shy about singing, Safia suggested that I take the tenth class, the matriculation group that would graduate that year, for English conversation. "The purpose is exactly the same—to expose the girls to foreign behavior and ideas in as positive a way as possible. They also need to listen to someone other than their teachers. We speak English as a second language, and they need to become comfortable with different accents."

These were the sixteen- and seventeen-year olds, who would be marrying or starting work or going on to college when they finished that year. Or, if they failed the government matriculation exams, they would repeat the year. Most of these girls had never been to a movie or a library unchaperoned, had never attended a concert or a play or driven a car, had never had a date with a young man.

But they were making serious plans for their futures. I asked the science section of my matric class what they hoped to do after school, and every one of them intended to go to college and become a doctor.

Thinking I hadn't understood, I inquired, "Will any of you study nursing?"

"No." Very positive.

"Why not?"

"Nursing is for men. We will be doctors."

"Every one of you?"

Nods from all thirty-seven of them. This in spite of the fact that they had no laboratory in which to work. The other section, who were not science majors, planned to enter teaching, social work, or home economics.

They were all so confident about where they were going, in spite of the fact that their school building was inadequate, with a very limited library and little else. Rooms were barely large enough to hold the classes, and some of the classrooms were simply areas separated by screens. The secondary school met only in the morning, making way in the afternoon for another complete shift of primary children. The furniture was crude but serviceable; much of it had been purchased out of Safia's salary when she took over the running of the school ten years before. The few pictures on the walls were pages cut from magazines, and the girls carefully read discarded periodicals and maps collected from the American community. Educational material from the USIS and the British Council was treasured and displayed on bulletin boards. Each classroom boasted only one small panel of blackboard and almost no other visual aids.

When I asked Safia how she came to her position, she said she had been chosen by a group of public-spirited citizens to run the school. Given the job, run it she did—from finding funds and teachers to balancing the budget, tending to maintenance, and deciding how much she herself could be paid. There were no school boards or PTAs to help her. Needless to say, her salary hardly reflected the amount of time and effort involved in making this undertaking a success.

After leaving Karachi, I kept in touch with Safia for several years, but finally the Christmas cards petered out. Twenty years later, we went back to Pakistan on a two-month assignment. The first day that the team did not need the car and driver, I knew exactly where I wanted to go.

"New Town Girls' School."

Karim looked over the back of the seat at me in surprise. He'd never heard of it.

"Well, take me to New Town. I'll find it."

So we drove out Motilal Road, and I spotted the familiar turns until we came up to the curb in front of the iron gate.

"It's not called that now," Karim informed me. "It's a public school."

"That's all right. You wait here."

I got out and went through the iron gates. The banyan trees still cast their huge pool of shade, and the familiar one-story building appeared between them at the end of the drive. The compound was deserted.

I walked across the hard-packed dirt that had been the volleyball court to what I remembered as the caretaker's cottage, and found an old woman there.

"I'm looking for Safia Khan."

This grizzled custodian spoke very little English, but she recognized the name, and indicated that Safia wasn't there.

"Is she in Karachi?"

The head nodded.

"Can you send her a message?"

Another nod.

So I wrote my name and the fact that I was staying at the Sind Club on a piece of notebook paper and gave it to the old woman. Then I walked back across the brown earth and under the banyan trees through a crowd of ghosts, who helped me open the tall iron gate and depart.

Three days later Safia phoned the Sind Club and came to tea. She was heavier now, and the black hair shot with gray. Same sweet smile, same gentle voice, same gracefully draped sari.

She told me that the government had nationalized all the schools in Pakistan. She had opposed this move, believing that private schools could play a useful role in her country. She was prominent enough in education circles that her opposition was well publicized. When the nationalization took place, she was dismissed from her position at New Town Girls' School, and had been denied any work in education ever since.

We talked till twilight in the big wicker chairs on the broad shadowy verandah of the Sind Club, filling in many years and covering many subjects. Before she left I learned that she had joined an opposition party because she so strongly opposed the dictatorial military government, and that her aged mother, whom she had supported for so many years, was no longer living.

I asked her what she was doing now. Her answer was a little vague, but she told me that the Iranian embassy was recruiting Pakistanis to teach English in Iran, and she had applied for one of the positions.

Langenscheidt's Lilliput Dictionary

Mary Rutkovsky-Ruskin

I had been living in Uskudar, Turkey, for a little less than a month when I began to experience an odd heaviness in my abdomen. I decided to visit the American hospital in Istanbul to make sure all was well.

After only a short wait, I was shown into the doctor's office. She asked what was wrong, I related my symptoms to her, and was pushed and prodded during an examination. She then invited me to have a seat in her office and asked how long I had been in Turkey and if I liked Uskudar. "After all," she said with a slight smile. "Uskudar is not Istanbul." I said yes, it was true, but it wasn't Uskudar that was difficult to adjust to, it was the entire country. Then she asked if I had anyone I could express my feelings to. I said yes, that I was married and my husband and I related very well. At that, she nodded and quickly scribbled something on a pad of paper. As she handed it to me, she said, "This isn't a prescription, per se, I'm just writing it down in case there's a language problem." She nodded efficiently and then rose from her chair.

I looked at the paper, unable to decipher what she had written. "What . . ." I began.

"If you have any problems, please come back." She opened the door for me.

Mary Rutkovsky-Ruskin's short stories and poems have been published in a variety of literary magazines and anthologies. She is presently working on her third novel, *The Wayward Quests of a Modern Candide*. Ms. Rutkovsky-Ruskin has lived in Istanbul, Paris, and on a small island in Greece. She presently resides in Manhattan.

"What is it that you're recommending I take?" I asked as we stood at the threshold of her office.

"It's just a laxative," she said with a withered smile. "Please come back if you have any problems."

I stood in the hallway and stared at the closed door. A laxative? I looked around. The shiny linoleum floors, antiseptic smells, and the cool and measured orderliness brought me back to grammar school. The tiny piece of paper in my hand reminded me of Mrs. Winiger's bathroom permission slips.

It was true—my symptoms probably were related to the fact that I wasn't finding life in Uskudar exactly easy. I looked at the clock on the wall. It had a huge round face with large numbers, the kind of clock one sees in classrooms, auditoriums, and public institutions. I came to the conclusion that it was not a good idea to visit a doctor near lunchtime.

"Well?" my husband asked, taking me by the arm. "Are you okay?"

"I guess so. She says I'm constipated."

Richard's shoulders collapsed. "Constipated!?" he said. "Is that all?"

"Shhhhh!" I said. "Not so loud!"

"Constipated?" he repeated in a whisper.

"Would it make you feel better if I had something more serious? Would you rather I had an exotic disease, like tronchozoa?"

"No, no, of course not!"

He looked at the piece of paper in my hand. "Is that her prescription?"

"It's an over-the-counter laxative. She wrote it down in case we have language problems."

We then proceeded to the pharmacy, conveniently located across the street.

I handed the pharmacist the piece of paper. He squinted as he tried to pronounce the word, which was comprised of twelve or thirteen letters.

"Vren—" he began, looking at us helplessly.

"It's a laxative," my husband explained in English.

"Lax-a-tif? What is the problem?" the pharmacist asked in Turkish.

Richard and I looked at each other. "How do you say constipated in Turkish?" he whispered. "I didn't bring my dictionary."

I reached into my handbag and handed him the Langenscheidt's Lilliput Turkish-English Dictionary I always carried but never used. He flipped through its minuscule pages.

"This is useless. It only translates from Turkish into English, not English into Turkish!" He handed it back to me. "If I knew the word in Turkish, I wouldn't need a dictionary in the first place."

"I knew something so tiny couldn't be practical," I said as I tucked the book back into my handbag.

The pharmacist cleared his voice. "Vren—?" He looked at me and then Richard. "Who is ill?" he asked in Turkish.

Richard pointed to me and in Turkish replied, "My wife."

"I'm not ill, Richard. I'm just constipated. Or at least that's what she thinks."

"What is the problem?" asked the pharmacist.

"She can't . . ." my husband began quietly. His cheeks turned a soft pink color.

"She can't?" the pharmacist repeated.

"She can't go," he blurted out in his uncertain Turkish.

The pharmacist looked at me compassionately. "Where can't she go?"

My husband and I glanced at one another, crestfallen. I didn't know whether to laugh or cry. Richard sighed. "He doesn't speak English, and for the life of me I can't think of the Turkish word for bathroom. Bathroom, bathroom. I can't believe it—my mind's gone completely blank! Bathroom—it's the first word we learned!"

"Wait," the pharmacist said. "I will get my boss. He knows English."

We both sighed with relief. The boss came out of the back room, smiling benignly.

Richard cleared his throat and in broken Turkish said, "We live here one month. Don't know Turkish well." If only we hadn't been so busy with our work, which required us to speak English and very little Turkish.

"I know English," the boss said proudly.

"You do? Wonderful," Richard began. "You see, my wife's constipated and needs a laxative. We've just come from the hospital." He waved to the hospital across the street. "The doctor suggested that she take a laxative," Richard added.

The boss shook his head and in Turkish said, "I know English, but not that well."

"Lax-a-tif," the pharmacist said to the boss.

"Lax-a-tif," the boss repeated with a meaningless shrug of his shoulders. "No lax-a-tif."

There was a moment of disappointed silence. Then the boss said, "Wait here. I find someone." He strode out the door, his gait full of purpose and resolution.

"Good," I said to Richard as we both watched him. "He's fetching someone." All three of us watched as the boss stopped a passerby who shook his head and walked on. "He's asking strangers if they speak English," Richard whispered.

"That's exactly what he's doing," I said in disbelief.

In a few minutes the boss ushered in an impeccably well-dressed man. "This gentleman knows English!" he announced in Turkish as he placed the man in front of us. "Speak, please!" he said to my husband.

"Constipation," Richard said. "Laxative." The pharmacist handed the well-dressed man the slip of paper.

"Vren—" began the man. "What is this?" he asked in a thickly accented English.

"Laxative," Richard and I repeated together.

"Lax-a-tif?" He straightened his shoulders and gave Richard a queer look. "I am very sorry I can not be of service," he said, putting the paper on the counter. He turned around and quickly left.

"Maybe he knew what it was but was too well-bred to admit it," I whispered to Richard.

"Or maybe it's one of those words that carry a double meaning," Richard said with a grin. The boss dashed out the door again, undaunted.

"Look, he's getting another one," Richard said. "We've got to stop him. Let's find a pharmacy that speaks English." We went outside and approached the boss, who by now was halfway down the block.

"We must go!" Richard called out to him in Turkish. "Thank you!"

"Wait!" the boss insisted. "Wait! I will find the man for you! Here he is!" He stopped another pedestrian. "English! Do you speak English?" he urgently asked in Turkish.

"Of course," replied the man, in Turkish.

"Then speak to them!"

"Yes? May I help you?" the man asked in faltering and stilted English.

"Constipation. Laxative," Richard said.

"Yes? May I help you?" he repeated.

"My wife is constipated."

I marveled at my husband's patience.

"Constipated?" The man looked at us blankly.

Another passerby entered our little circle. "Constipated?" he repeated.

"You know it?" the boss asked him in Turkish.

"Pfut," the man said with an uplift of his chin.

A man stepped out of a car and joined us. Then another man appeared. And another. The boss explained our dilemma to each newcomer in rapid-fire Turkish. Everyone spoke at once. Suddenly, the entire crowd of men became silent. They stared at the ground and shook their heads.

One of the men touched my husband's arm enthusiastically. He pantomimed a person vomiting. "Yes?" he asked us. "Yes?" The crowd became excited.

"No," we said. "No." The crowd was dismayed.

Next, the man hugged himself, as if he were cold. "Yes? Yes?"

"No. No."

He fanned himself with his hand, as if he were hot. "Yes?"

"No," we both replied.

"What, then?" he asked hopelessly. "What? Show us!"

My husband looked at me. "I don't believe this," he muttered. By now, a very large crowd had gathered.

"Show us!" the crowd called out. "Show us!"

Richard smiled weakly at me and turned to the group of men. He made a gesture as if he were eating. Then he traced the food down his esophagus, through the small intestines and down into the large intestines. He pretended to sit on a toilet. He held his stomach, groaned, and waved his hands helplessly. In between groans, he muttered, "Tell me I'm not really doing this." When his performance was over, we both anxiously awaited a verdict.

Everyone spoke at once. "Lax-a-tif," they said. "Con-sti-pa-tion." "A problem." "What does it mean?" Some removed their caps and scratched their heads, in that timeless international gesture. A number of them tsked and clucked sympathetically.

"I was never very good at charades," Richard whispered as we waited for the outcome.

Just then, a group of workers rounded the corner. The boss called out to Richard in Turkish, *"Efendi,* sir, show them! Perhaps they understand English!"

"Yes, show them!" repeated the crowd.

"We must go," Richard said as he perused the band of jovial workers.

"We must help you!" the crowd called out.

"No, we must go," Richard repeated. We slowly inched our way in the direction of the bus stop. "Thank you for your help!"

"Efendi!" they shouted. "Come back, my friends, come back!"

As we walked rapidly away from the chattering crowd, I grinned mischievously at my husband. "Richard, we'd better hurry."

"Now what?"

"I have to go the bathroom!"

Echoes of Guilt

Sue Jaffee

L istening to her, I tried to visualize an innocent hill tribe baby mutilated, thrashed to death against a boulder near the edge of the jungle in Thailand. The tea I was trying to sip had no soothing effect. Certainly, Ira was not downing the Singha (beer) with his usual gusto. You could say that the sick feeling I had came from knowing about this act of brutality taking place in the jungle. Somehow the harshness of it all was magnified because of an indefinable silence that exists there. You soon begin to sense clearly the injustice of life, and yes, the injustice of death. Ever since our honeymoon to Botswana, I had wanted to think of jungles, regardless of location, as nothing less than alluring, but obviously that's a fool's romantic dream. Poaching of animals was one thing, but the taking of human life was another.

We had walked into town to buy a few lacquerware boxes before our departure for home the next evening. Walking from the hospital complex to the night bazaar had become an evening ritual for us. Ira had nicknamed me the queen of the night bazaar; the merchants and the hawkers knew us by sight, and always appeared very happy to see us, happier still to take our money.

We couldn't help but notice her when we sat down—she was striking. You could feel her presence in a mysterious way. "She's staring at us. I wonder who she is."

Sue Jaffee is a former teacher of writing and literature and is now a freelance writer. Her work has appeared in the *AMA News*, *The St. Petersburg Times*, the *Miami News*, and she coauthored, with her husband, a health care book for rural women.

Ira's eyes were fixed, "I have no idea."

I was intrigued by her as well. "She looks like a French model, or perhaps she is on location—maybe a Vietnam movie is being filmed here."

"You might be right. There's lush scenery, particularly around the Golden Triangle. Probably economically feasible to do as much work as possible in Thailand."

"Her appeal is that she is truly beautiful without being heavily painted."

She approached us.

"Do you mind terribly if I join you?"

Before we could utter a word, "I could not help overhearing your American accents."

I wondered what else she had overheard.

"I'm lonely for people from home, as I've been in the Akha village for over a year."

As soon as she said Akha, I recognized that it was one of the seven Thai hill tribe settlements. God, I thought to myself, that's the most primitive one, from what I've read. What is she doing there?

"Are you touring in Thailand?"

"Not exactly. We've been working as volunteers at McCormick Hospital here in Chiang Mai."

She put out her hand to both of us.

"I'm a missionary. Originally from California. It has been rewarding serving the Lord and yet difficult here. I mean really difficult. I have to live with something that I'm afraid is going to haunt me the rest of my life. Something that happened in the village."

There was a long silence. I wondered who was going to speak first.

Her eyes started to fill with tears. "A young hill tribe girl in our village came to me begging in the only way that she knew how for me to take her baby. Under the law I couldn't adopt her baby because I have two children of my own. That's Thai law, you know. Her name is Petachyara, only fourteen. For her the shame is tremendous, not being married. I awake at night seeing her baby girl wrapped in the *phakama*, loincloth, so tiny, so delicate. She was only a few days old when my husband discovered her little body while hunting. I can still hear Petachyara pleading with me. Haven't told anyone of this. As you know, where I am it's quite isolated. I came here to the guest house to be alone with the Lord. I'm hoping He will give me some answers as to what I should do."

"Do you think Petachyara killed her own baby?" I asked.

"Yes, I feel so as she's now nowhere to be found, but I somehow believe she could have fled to Bangkok."

"Why Bangkok?" Ira asked. "For all you know you might find her here in Chiang Mai. A lot of the hill tribe people come here to the night bazaar to sell their wares."

"Chiang Mai is too near to the villages. It would be too obvious—she wouldn't stay here. Besides, there's a much better prostitution market in Bangkok. The young girls are really exploited. Out of the village she has no means of survival at this point unless she's selling her body. I fear going to the authorities as my husband and I could be accused of the murder."

All I could say was, "We create our own destiny. I don't know how much this has to do with religion. But Petachyara committed the act. You didn't kill her baby. You only know the truth as it pertains to you."

We embraced her and walked away slowly. At the end of the cobblestone path, we waved.Her face was sad.

We went to bed early that night. I could not sleep. Thoughts raced to Petachyara, to ads I had seen in the local paper for massage parlors in Bangkok, to days of growing up in the hills of West Virginia. I could see myself in Sunday school and later attending church services, listening to the choir bellowing "Onward Christian Soldiers" and "The Old Rugged Cross," and even then wondering what all this meant.

Shanghai Diary

Layle Silbert

O n New Year's Eve, 1946, I arrived in Shanghai to be with
my husband, who had preceded me by a couple of months
to work for the United Nations Relief and Rehabilitation
Administration (UNRRA), which was helping rebuild countries
after the Second World War. This was a few years before the
current Chinese government came into power in China. Shanghai was full of all kinds of foreigners and English was fairly current. We lived in Shanghai for most of 1947.

Shanghai, January 29. It's a week since the Chinese New Year.
Before that were the Russian New Year and, of course, our very
own on January 1. Now there are no more coming up. Neither
do there seem to be any jobs for me. But at least looking for a
job is a way to learn a city. Unemployed I arrived and unemployed I remain, in the condition the State Department describes
as "housewife" on my passport, which I resent. We don't have a
house, just our room with the Golempolskys.

Some UNRRA wives who came over with me had jobs
waiting in UNRRA, usually as secretaries. I don't know how to
be a secretary and am glad I don't. There aren't many other
kinds of jobs around. Most logically I started looking at the U.S.
Information Service (USIS) in Hamilton House, that hybrid
office and apartment building in the very center of the city. A

Ms. Silbert has published more than fifty stories in literary magazines and
quarterlies, a book of stories, *Imaginary People and Other Strangers* (Exile Press,
1985) and a book of poems, *Making a Baby in Union Park Chicago* (Downtown
Poets, 1983). She is a freelance photographer, mostly of writers, and has had
more than thirty solo exhibits.

middle-aged man in shirtsleeves greeted me as if I were Miss America herself until I explained that I wasn't a stenographer. His face fell. No job. No money for staff positions.

When I got home that day, Abe was back from work early, waiting for me to get back too. Did I find a job? I explained. He looked more disappointed than I was. What if I don't find a job at all? We may never move. Any place we might find would cost more than Abe's rental allowance.

I haven't been without a full-time occupation since the day when I was five and a half years old and my father took me to school for the first time. I had to come to China to know idleness, to have the leisure to sit and look at our neighbors in the lane, learning their habits, observing. It's like a chapter in a novel.

February 3. I have a job, a part-time job. I am a professor of English conversation at the Shanghai National Institute of Commerce and have a document to prove it, a certificate with my name and "professor" standing out in a field of Chinese characters. Mr. Kuo, Abe's Chinese statistical assistant, obtained the work for me through his friend Mr. Chen, who also teaches at the institute, which is really a college.

The transaction took place in Abe's office in the Embankment Building as all statistical work stopped. Mr. Chen arrived in a long, loose mandarin gown, with an umbrella, his hair shaggy, in horn-rims. Mr. Kuo took charge with his ineffable knowing smile that says life is a joke. Around here much life is. Since his subject is English literature, Mr. Chen speaks English, but more haltingly than Mr. Kuo, who therefore was the one who explained the job.

I am to give students of English practice in speaking English. Then Mr. Chen spoke to Mr. Kuo in Chinese and Mr. Kuo explained further to me that my best qualification was my lack of knowledge of Chinese. It would preclude any cheating by me in Chinese.

Mr. Chen handed me the certificate. We shook hands. I thanked them each and went home to think about how to teach English conversation.

February 10. I had barely begun dispatching my duties as professor of English conversation when I had to take a leave of absence. Today I explained to Mr. Lee, the dean of students, that we are leaving on a tour of Canton and Hong Kong for the sake of Abe's work and he agreed amiably to hold the job for me. I don't think there are any other applicants anyway.

My students, who are, as promised, college seniors, have taken courses in English but speak the language atrociously. Sometimes I think their speech has more effect on me than my teaching on them as I catch myself speaking pidgin English. I have discovered that I am taking naturally to pidgin English, especially after somebody in the UNRRA mess explained its principles to be roughly like those of Chinese itself. I doubt it, but the idea helps.

The classrooms in the institute are unheated. So I stand in front of the students, who sit in the same rows of bolted-down desks as at *l'Université de l'Aurore,* wearing ski pants and my all-purpose stormcoat with the hood hanging ripely from the collar.

As I struggle to convey sounds of broken English while infecting the students with my midwest speech, and ask more questions than I thought I could ever invent in order to arouse responses, I am being watched. Through the glass in the upper part of the door, I am watched by other students and passing teachers, and through the windows by children staring, smiling, laughing with amusement at me. In the middle of this sophisticated city, my presence excites curiosity.

From the beginning, I've heard about the famous unbounded curiosity of the Chinese. To foreigners it feels personal. Some of them complain that the curiosity unnerves them, almost as much as the long-range spitting. A Chinese nurse told me that when she goes into rural areas to do public health work she is stared at by other Chinese herself. The curiosity is applied to all bona fide curiosities whether Chinese or foreign. Nobody teaches little Chinese children that it's bad manners to stare, and forever after they look and stare.

This is the first time I have attracted attention from so many, and with small surprise see I am not unnerved. I like being watched, or rather I like that I am being watched, because this is more of China pressing its nose on the glass. Like a drunkard, I crave experience. Maybe I envy them too, when I am obliged by who I am to do my staring furtively and inefficiently at the endless curiosities of my life here. Anyway, I have to go on with the teaching. My students do not mind the crowds outside, so why should I? Besides that, they are surely curious as well.

Another surprise is that I am not scared, scared to stand in front of these strangers, without an outline, instructions, textbook, curriculum, or precedent, and with only my wit and ingenuity to tell me what to do.

"And you were not frightened?" our landlady asked when I got back from the first session, her dark Russian eyes large with her fears for me in her plump young face.

"No, why should I be? I'm the teacher. I know my subject."

"Oh, you Americans," she said, as if to say, you want to teach the world. The suggestion horrified me. I went into our room and closed the door.

I'd felt only a casual sureness. "Good afternoon," I'd said boldly the first day, smiled and waited. "Good afternoon," they each said, distinctly.

I started. I connived, I schemed up devices for conversation and discourse, made explanations, wrote words on the blackboard, sent the students to the blackboard, asked cunning questions, now and then falling back on a joke. Jokes were the only device that fell flat.

In impasses I've been doing what works. I laugh and will my laughter to spread. It does and we all laugh. It is marvelous medicine. Then I start again.

Letters Home

Anne Dammarell

January 5, 1989

Dear Eliz,

I have just returned from Old Coptic Cairo, site of convents with relics of St. George. I witnessed a poor, very pregnant, and sick woman seek a blessing from the little, slightly deformed nun, who placed a heavy iron collar and chains on the woman who sought relief. I hope her faith cures her.

My apartment is wonderful. My initial reaction was "Oh, my God, how will I ever get this place clean?" I've spent two days on the kitchen and three on the bathrooms and am convinced that all is well. I've never SCRUBBED before. It's hard on the hands! After nearly suffocating myself on cleanser, two plumbers came to fix—you realize that I use the word "fix" loosely—the hot water in the shower, and managed to call forth from the depths of ancient Cairo two inches of gunk, which they tramped across the living room floor to the door. We're talking major gunk. I could only laugh. At least I can now take a hot shower. Really a wonderful thing. Now that the place is relatively clean (I'm obsessed with cleanliness), I'm trying to make it hospitable. The apartment is so big that trying to make it cozy

---

Anne Dammarell is a freelance writer living in Washington, D.C. After working twenty-three years with the Agency for International Development, she "retired" to Egypt to teach in a Coptic Catholic Seminary for two years. She is presently writing an account of her experiences in Lebanon where she survived the bombing of the Beirut Embassy in 1983.

is hard. It is a two bedroom with crystal and red-beaded Egyptian chandeliers. The place has a few *jinns*, prankish spirits. Light switches sometimes work. Hot water comes at will. The front door opens to the dining room, a dark, oblong room with a side wall oozing bubbly plaster. A smaller, square room off to the right gives way to a small balcony overlooking the street. It is my living room because it has sunlight in the morning. My bedroom has a large table that has become my "office," and two twin beds. The guest bedroom is next to mine and has a king-sized bed. One glance at the red and white bedboard explains why I have dubbed it the "Lucille Ball Room."

I have never worked so little and yet so hard. I simply have no time. Yet, when I read my journal, I see that I have done nothing! The Middle East has a pace of its own. Tonight I had been invited by an Egyptian couple to see the dervishes whirl. When I got there the entire family was gathered because their stepmother returned from the hospital that afternoon. After three and a half hours of tea and chatter, I grasped that plans had changed and we were not going to see the dervishes.

I've already broken a religious tabu. Three days after my arrival the American priest at church asked me to do the first reading at mass on Sunday. I asked if I should proceed in with him carrying the book overhead like they do at Dalghren Chapel at Georgetown University. He said, "Yes, and just sit down next to the lectern. Come up to the altar when I break up the host. We'll take communion together." Well, we weren't even fully in the sacristy after mass when a priest came running up whispering loudly, "Women are not allowed on the altar!" A lively Sudanese woman came up to me afterward, all smiles. "I like it. But women don't read here." Do you think they had to wash down the altar after I left?

I met an American woman named Fatimah. While I was having my space heater repaired (can't complain, it had worked for an entire two weeks), I heard an American woman speak fluent, god-awful Arabic. Out of courtesy to the homeland I didn't turn around, but when she came up to pay, I greeted her. She was startled to learn that I teach at Coptic Catholic seminary in Sakanat Maadi. She lives next door. I'm invited to her house for coffee. She is about my age, married to an Argentine and has lived here twenty years. She wanted me to teach a Saudi princess English. I declined. I asked Abuna Kamel, the head of

St. Leo's, about her. He raised his hands and eyes heavenly and shouted, "She gives much trouble!" She rents her villa from the seminary for 25LE ($12) a month and tries to convert them to Islam. I think I'm going to like this woman. I like Kamel. He is not at all what I thought he would be. He's very open. I have the feeling this city is paced with individuals. I'm trying to avoid taking them for granted, which is easy to do since just getting the basics together is so bizarre the odd people seem natural. For example, this morning I went up to the department store, Hanaux, for the February sale and was engulfed by a dozen women each representing an aspect of Cairo, from aged Francophiles to the up-to-date veiled coquette. If I simply described each, I'd have an article for the *New Yorker*.

I'm going to sign up for a two-day workshop at *Cairo Today*, a slick Egyptian magazine for the English community. The objective is organization of thoughts. Wouldn't it be horrid if I discover that it's thoughts I lack and not organization?

There are many things to do here. A new opera house has been donated by the Japanese. "Showboat" is scheduled for the end of the month. There are trips to the western oases and Yemen and unlimited lectures. I can see why people enjoy living here. Must go. Dogs are yapping and the woman above is running around in high heels on the wooden floors. It must be bedtime.

March 6, 1989

Dear Eliz,

My unconscious me knows Arabic but I do not. How else can I explain my tranquility as I blunder through Egypt. En route back from Shibeen in the Delta, I greeted the minibus driver with "happy sucking" rather than "good afternoon." He responded with a worried look rather than the expected *"Mas el nour."** Twice a week, I go to Mohandiseen for Survival Arabic at the International Language Institute. I can now say "My name is Anne. I'm from America." I tell all the taxi drivers that

---

*literally, "may the light shine upon you"; good afternoon

I'm from Ireland so as not to disgrace my country by an accidental foul comment. I am studying the Arabic alphabet on my own using a text designed for illiterate five-year old Egyptians. A major drawback is not knowing what the word means. Some have pictures so I am reasonably sure of those: lion, camel, rose. Some say Arabic is a hard language. I find it fun, an excellent substitute for the *New York Times'* crossword puzzle.

My English classes may produce future Naguib Mahfouzs. Philosophy II students now write five-sentence essays! The concept of a beginning, a middle, and an end seems to have rooted. The madames of the Sacred Heart did have an effect on me after all. A la Mother Mouton, I give an opening line and for homework my students continue the story using the particular tense studied during class. "The seminarians have run off to Brazil!" kicked off the present perfect essay. The first two seminarians delivered lively little pieces about playing football with Pele and drinking coffee. Downhill after that. The last one spoke about going to Rio to eat foul and "pray the mass."

My intellectual life ain't. An American friend got me hooked on "Knot's Landing." It comes on every night at 9:15. Real trash and I love it. I get angry now when my dinner guests don't leave at 9:00 P.M., which of course they never do.

A parting note: A French archaeologist claims to have found an extraterrestrial refrigerated inside a secret chamber of a pyramid. It must be true—I read it in the newspaper.

April 11, 1989

Dear Eliz,

We now live in the thick of real Egyptian weather—hot. Closed shutters hot. Rooms darkened to the feel of an attic in a heavy noonday sun that coats dusty Cairo. Spring left abruptly three days ago as if to avoid Ramadan. A single bird chatters outside my balcony. An occasional horn toot toots a warning, presumably at a pedestrian or a dog ambling down a street narrowed by double-parked cars. The tomcat next door whines like a petulant two-year old. Air conditioners of the U.S. marines across the way hum in that wonderfully consistent, grandmotherly way air conditioners hum on scorching Washington days. No people sounds. Muslims have started their month-long sacred fast. No water, no food, no sex, no smoking, from sunup to sundown. The cannon from atop the Citadel booms the start and end of the fast each day. *Iftar,* breakfast, begins about 6:00 in the evening. When I first heard the canon I thought, "A coup d'etat!" I was crossing the Nile enroute to mass at St. Joseph's in Zamalek yesterday evening and managed to forget that Cairo hosts fifteen million people. I walked down the middle of Tahrir Bridge without having to dodge donkey carts and cars "knitting" lanes. The few taxis hurrying home for *iftar* swerved around me. Tired policemen still dressed in winter black crowded together to catch the shade of their pointed roof guard box. An old man in the ubiquitous pale green *galabya,* traditional robe, propped himself against a straggly tree waiting to drink water from an old Baraka plastic bottle lying at his side. I respect those who fast. Just the thought of no water in this heat defeats me.

One of my upper-level students, Gamel, told me that his cousin died. A mother of three, she died in childbirth (she was twenty-one). A good woman, he said, a poor woman. He did not know how to answer the village lament: "Why did God do this?" Gamel didn't know the reason for her death. Nor could he come up with any of the standard possibilities: early marriage, frequent pregnancies, poor hygiene, unclean water, limited nutrition, lack of medical facilities, chronic fatigue. I began to wonder what the seminarians knew of the lot of women. As priests, they will have tremendous influence. I decided to have Dr. Azziz Khattab address the students. I must admit to some apprehension. A Moslem talking about sensitive issues dealing with women in a Coptic Catholic seminary could have run into a few snags. The lecture, major health problems faced by Egyptian women, went well. The seminarians listened so intently they forgot to doodle or to laugh at silent exchanges of fellow captives. Female circumcision, horrid and unhealthy, fascinating and repulsive, demands attention. Khattab knows his audience. He led with a description of operating procedures used among poor folk—Christian and Moslem—to remove the clitoris of the preadolescent. Not a pretty story. For me the notion surpasses the physical act. The concept that a woman's body needs correction violates the concept of God and the value of women. I understand from reading (not personal conversations) that all women remember the pain and bewilderment, but only a few question the rational and the morality. After all, a woman must marry, and few men want an uncircumcised woman. When I phoned to thank Dr. Khattab, he said he'd had an hour of questions and comments after the formal talk. (I'd gone for fear of inhibiting the free flow of questions.) His talk had an effect on me too. I heard a child shrieking early this morning, screaming furiously and long. My immediate reaction to the cries was to wonder if the child were a girl.

CHAPTER 4

IMAGES IN VERSE

Interlude, Afghanistan

Elisavietta Ritchie

In the cave we drink cardamom tea,
crack pistachio nuts,
eat honey cakes.

The fire in the stones burns low.
Beyond the cave mouth the sky
prickles with stars.

We tell one another tales.
From your eyes I think
there is more you want to say

but sudden planes roar ahead—
Shots resound in the hills—
Flares extinguish the stars.

A Writer Named Fatimah

Elisavietta Ritchie

Penang, Malaysia

She suffers for all beaten creatures;

yoked oxen hauling logs across the ruts,
spinal ridges taller than a man,
heads bent toward dust,

while from the broken cart their master
whacks them forward with a board
until their old sores bleed;

she also pities him, shirt torn,
skin leathered like those hides,
as he flails at the flies, and knows

he'll move no faster up the road
than oxen walk and Allah wills,
and drought comes every year;

she sorrows for his hungry sons,
composes stories they'll never read
and tries to tell them what they might become.

She would embrace the poor of all the earth
and mourns because she can't.
She saves a kitten with a crooked tail.

Only for herself she shows no pity:
All day she teaches, but how many learn?
All night she writes, but who will buy?

For those who would embrace her,
she draws limits on the love she'll take,
would hide her passion in her lines.

She loves a god who asks no pity, only servitude.

Elisavietta Ritchie's seven collections include the award-winning *Raking the Snow* and *Tightening the Circle Over Eel Country*. Four of her stories have been the PEN Syndicated Fiction winners. The U.S. Information Agency sponsored her as a visiting poet abroad. She has read at the Library of Congress and many other places.

The Subramuniyam Temple

Geoffrey Cook

A high hill
    overlooking the South Indian plain
Lord Subramuniyam Temple / on crest
   son of Shiva and Paravati
A yogi sits in a cave below
   meditating for 4,000 years
   maintaining the holy place
1,008 steps to inner sanctum
Through the portico
   a beggar baby screams
     flies eat his eyes

Bombay

Geoffrey Cook

Gateway to India
        Holy India
Sun rising from the coastal lowlands
humid breeze off the Arabian Sea
Smell of burning cow shit
Paper shack houses
        myriad shacks
People too poor for shacks
        sleeping on sidewalks
                hundreds
                        thousands
        waking
        millions walking
                riding bicycles
Bus / racing
        honking
        dodging Brahmin bulls
people jumping to side of road
Small girl pounding stomache
        begging . . .

New Delhi Intercontinental Hotel

Geoffrey Cook

Humid, hot Delhi afternoon
Guests swim in pool
    from air-conditioned lobby
Silk-saried women cross deep carpet
Indian businessmen chatter over London Stock Exchange
    and stability of American dollar
Old beggar woman
    exposing leprosy-gnawed limb
    stare through window
    whimpering:
    "Bapu!"*

*Father

Geoffrey Cook is a poet, translator, literary critic, and visual artist. At thirty-five he decided to be a scholar, too. He now has his master's degree from the University of California at Berkeley and is struggling toward a doctoral degree.

Anyanhaseyo Ajumoni —
Hello, Auntie in Korean

Hilary Tham

They told me I would see white granite
Buddhas, temples, the hill mound graves
of kings, cherry blossoms in the Land
of the Morning Clouds. They did not mention
shipping crate hovels and burlap
curtain doors, street bodies asleep
along the outside walls of houses.
Ajumoni said many died last winter,
"Government think help them: fix low price
for coal briquettes. Merchants mix clay
dirt. Poor people but cheapest thing,
they not get warm, they die from poison smoke."

Ajumoni, "Auntie" (we never knew her name)
came with the group house we shared
with ten Peace Corps volunteers, rented from
Sogong University. We suspected her visitors left
with paper bags of our rice; she always needed
more money for food. When we protested, she
fed us soy sauce noodles or sesame leaves
fried in batter with plain rice.
"Meat is costing much," she'd say.
Being carnivores, we capitulated,
increased her food allowance.
She was a good housekeeper, always
cleaning or cooking or chopping white

cabbage to sprinkle with cayenne and salt,
packing them into clay jars to bury
by the garden for winter *kimchi.*

One predawn, awakened by a sound, I saw her
making stacks of peanut butter sandwiches
which disappeared as a band of boys
in school uniforms trooped silently
through our kitchen. "My cousins' sons,"
Ajumoni said without shame. "I give them
American helping. Now they like Americans
very much."

When autumn came, we left Korea. Ajumoni
stood in the doorway, sorry to see us go,
she said. Looking back from the taxi, I saw
her thin face, black hair pulled into a bun
on her nape, her hands already busy with a broom
to make ready the house for new renters, ready
to dispense foreign aid on their behalf.

Hilary Tham is a naturalized American from Malaysia who grew up with a god in every corner and a mother who had a superstition for everything. She is the author of *Tigerbone Wine, Bad Names for Women, Paper Boats,* and *No Gods Today.* Her poetry has been published in *Antietam Review, Pulpsmith, Wind, Gargoyle, Pig Iron, Poet Lore,* and others.

Ndutu

Sue Jaffee

The Masai claimed you, and your name belongs to them.
Legend whispers through translation that you are a peaceful
        place.
I attest to that truth as you offer solace to the weary traveler.
Your lake provides inspiration where birds are invited to
        bellow loudly nature's purest medley.
No words are necessary as here I am surrounded by visual
        poetry.

Whose Bargain?

Sue Jaffee

"Jamba," echoes from every stand. Hello.
"Come Mama, see the Makonde carvings."
"You are invited to look around."
The sun shines brightly.
The air does not move inside the market.

I feel the adrenaline pumping.
I know I've fallen prey.
I reply, "Mama is just looking about."
You must understand that in Tanzania I'm Mama, not Madame.

Competition starts to swell as I touch, admire, and compare.
The negotiation transcends the cultural tide as I confront my
    gut instinct while testing my conscience and theirs.

I say to myself, think shillings to dollars—dollars to shillings.
On whose terms will the last bid be made?
Will I walk leaving behind art that is an integral part of them?
Should I feel guilt for haggling in a Third World country?
Perhaps yes—perhaps no.
After all, in business nothing goes for free.

Each of us is present to negotiate.
Just maybe the deal will produce an exchange that will be a
    gift for both worlds to share.
There will be no loser.

Sue Jaffee is a former teacher of writing and literature and is now a freelance writer. Her work has appeared in the *AMA News,* the *St. Petersburg Times,* the *Miami News,* and she co-authored, with her husband, a health care book for rural women.

First Impressions

Elayne Clift

A sky turned upside down,
With cotton clouds hovering under foot above the valley,
Tropical flowers of fuschia, gold and orange,
And locusts like giant grasshoppers.
Women with bundles on their heads and babies on their backs,
A sea of saris and sweatshirts and African headresses
Flowing like a river into the campus of Nairobi University,
And everywhere
Beautiful, beautiful black faces smiling in welcome.

And Still the Women Weep

Elayne Clift

In the village,
Men gather
To hear the extension worker
Talk about growing good crops,

And still the women plant.

In the market,
Men sit
In tea shops talking about
Water and
Deciding who gets a well,

And still the women fetch.

In the city,
Men meet
To argue over budgets
And projects for
Income generation,

And still the women weave.

In the capital,
Men convene
To plan policy
For child survival
And "maternal health,"

And still the women tend.

In the august institutions of the world,
Men come together
To debate "development"
In the name
Of all the others,

And still the women weep.

Elayne Clift is a writer and health communications consultant in Potomac, Maryland. Her collected essays, *Telling It Like It Is: Reflections of a Not So Radical Feminist* (KIT, Inc.), appeared in 1991.

For Sonia

Sybil Smith

L ast night I bathed
for the first time in five days
and trembled with the pleasure of it.
I thought of you, Sonia,
of the El Rosario dirt, shit,
sweat, particulate matter
sluicing from my skin, tanned
from the Honduran sun
but still white, white
and trembling to be clean
and turn the handles on
instead of squatting in a stream
near where the cattle cross,
as I've seen you,
your thin brown back
turned to the road.

We've worked together
for five days.
You are so quick and slim,
and though I cannot tell you
what I think,
we are comfortable,
two women.

I imagined you in the shower with me,
and Dunia, too, 3, like my child.

And Alba, your brother's wife,
so plump and gay.
I imagined us all together
under the spray
the dirt and pain of El Rosario
washing away
around our feet, our laughter
bouncing against the tiles.

So now I know
I will never forget you.
Quick and slim I see you
crossing the Rio Grande
to join your husband
illegal already
in the land of plenty
from which I came
to know you. I see you crossing
lithe and brown,
holding Dunia with one hand,
and with the other
holding a bundle
on your head.

Godspeed, sister, friend.

For Marta

Sybil Smith

Remember, Marta, my knee,
how you laid your head
against my knee.
Remember that I was soft,
that you leaned into me,
and I held you, lice and all.
Remember that I was clean
and you dirty,
but we were both warm finally,
huddled together in the wet wind.
I had seen you crouched
in the lee of my tent,
knee to chest,
whispering in Spanish,
making washing, washing motions
with your hands.
And I saw you were the one
whose knotted hair I'd combed,
and whose face and hands I'd cleaned
the day before.
And here you were again.

One blanket, my group insists,
is not enough.
Don't give away things,
you make beggars.
But what would Christ have done?

I wanted to scream at them,
to scream at the sky.

Instead I did what is left
when nothing is left,
I held you close
against my body.

                      •

When I shook
you may have thought
it was the wind.
Perhaps my tears the rain.

Or is the gringa crying?

Esta bien, Marta, esta bien.
Till the wind blows you away,
let my body be your blanket
for a time.

Sybil Smith was born and educated in Vermont, but has traveled widely as a nurse. Her poems have appeared in numerous publications including *New England Review/Bread Loaf Quarterly, Southern Poetry Review, Cumberland Poetry Review, New Virginia Review,* and *Spoon River Quarterly.* Her fiction and non-fiction has appeared in *Spectrum, The Albany Review, Ithaca Women's Anthology, Northern Review, Ellipsis,* and *Vermont Woman.* Fiction is upcoming in an anthology titled *Back in My Body.* She lives in Vermont with her husband and daughter, and works as a psychiatric nurse.

To order additional copies of this book, photocopy this coupon and send payment (check or money order) to:

Elayne Clift
OGN Publications

11320 Rouen Drive, Potomac, Maryland 20854

Please send me:

Qty	Title	Price ea.	Total
___	**But Do They Have Field Experience!**	$14.95	____
		Subtotal	____
	Shipping and Handling ($1/book)		____
		Total	____

Name _____

Address _____

City/State _____ Zip _____

Phone No. *(in case we have questions about your order)* _____